Seven Days in Silence

How to find oneself in quiet meditation

Stephan Bielfeldt

Seven Days in Silence

How to find oneself in

quiet meditation

Translated by Robert Watson

Bibliographic information published by the
Deutsche Nationalbibliothek:

The Deutsche Nationalbibliothek lists this publication in
the Deutsche Nationalbibliografie; detailed bibliographic
data are available on the Internet at http://dnb.dnb.de.

Production and publishing: BoD - Books on Demand,
Norderstedt, Germany

ISBN: 9783758325663

For Toni

Content

Foreword 9

Acknowledgements 11

Introduction 13

The First Evening 18

Day 1: What is Meditation? 31

Day 2: Feelings 45

Day 3: Ego Mind 61

Day 4: What Sustains Us? 77

Day 5: Conflict and Decision Making 91

Day 6: Awareness in Everyday Life 111

Postscript 130

Recommended Books and Contacts 137

Bibliography 141

About the Author 143

Foreword

Many years ago, I went to a workshop on Non-Violent Communication. Participants performed little sketches in which they found themselves caught up in emotionally stressful situations. It was an exercise in not giving in to one's learned impulses (for example, blaming others), but rather in giving a voice to that sensitivity that is always present within.

It was in this workshop that I came to realize that most people have no idea what their feelings are in the moment. Instead, they often describe a complex mixture of feelings, concepts and patterns of reactions that determine our words and actions at any given moment. How can we change anything when we are not even aware of what "is"?

It is this possibility of finding out what really "is" that Stephan Bielfeldt brings into focus in his talks. For him, meditation means being still and quiet before one's self and others, with respect and with dignity. It means cultivating a way of looking and seeing that allows us to learn how we can better know who we are and understand that which makes us content and brings happiness. With intelligence and unassumingly he finds a way of creating an atmosphere of clarity and intensity that is very much his own.

He constantly arouses one's curiosity rather than giving ready answers, and proposes that we undertake a voyage of discovery without knowing where it will lead and without knowing what we may discover. With knowledge and clarity of insight, Stephan confronts the challenges that present themselves in this work. We are creatures of our genes, but we can change and accept full responsibility for our actions. His is a creative approach, and in different ways shows us how, through meditation, we may become aware of the many contradictions in our lives and how we can come to trust that which comes out of the work of meditation. You can sense that he is speaking from personal experience, and feel his joy at sharing it with others.

Dagmar Apel

April 2023

Acknowledgements

I want to thank my wife, Sabine, who has been by my side from the very beginning of my meditation work. She has been my faithful partner in the countless conversations about the work of meditation and about this book. After she had transcribed the recordings of the talks herein presented, she convinced me that they belonged between the covers of a book: it would not have come into being without her steadfast support and encouragement.

My thanks go out to my friend, Joachim Stueben, for his most helpful suggestions about the content and lay-out of the book. His professional over-sight of the German edition was a great help and a big thankyou to Stacey McQuade for reviewing the English edition.

I want to thank Joan Tollifson for reading the manuscript and giving me advice how to publish in the USA and UK.

My thanks go out also to Dagmar Apel for her beautiful foreword. Her enthusiasm for the project was a great source of encouragement to me.

My thanks to everyone who works and teaches at Springwater, which has become my spiritual home since the death of Toni Packer.

The seven-day retreat described in the book took place at the Seminarhaus Schlagsuelsdorf. I am grateful to everyone there for the warm welcome they extended to us.

My special thanks to the many people who took part in this and other seven-day retreats and who spoke with me in private meetings and took part in the group dialogues. I often think that I have learned more from them than they from me, such was their practical advice and especially their openness and trust. It is a pleasure for me to be able to give something back by means of this book.

It is a huge gift to me that a man of great understanding of the meditation work translated this book into English. I am very grateful to my dear friend Robert Watson for creating this English edition.

Introduction

"No talking for a whole week? I can't even imagine doing something like that!" I always hear people say that when I talk about my seven-day silent retreats. When you don't know something first hand, all sort of imaginings come up. But what is it really like to spend a whole week in silence, and why would one do it? In this book, I have set myself the task of introducing both people who have never meditated before and those who have already worked in various other traditions, to this free and open, non-traditional way of meditating.

The outer aspect is easy to describe: a small group of ten to thirty people come together in order to spend several days in stillness and silence. People of all backgrounds and traditions are welcome. Neither age nor health may be invoked as a reason not to meditate in this manner. You may adopt any posture you like, as your body allows, so that there is no strain on you as you meditate.

Retreats are at least four days in length but never more than ten, and take place in quiet surroundings, in a building where it is possible to remain in silence for the duration of the retreat. This means that we are in silence throughout the building and when we go outside. We come together to meditate, in a big room set aside for that purpose. We meditate in silence, but then all of our daily activities take place in silence – mealtimes, rest periods and also when we go for walks outside. When we come together to meditate, we sit on mats or benches or in chairs, but no particular posture is recommended, as is the case in other traditions. Everyone chooses the position that works best, and you are allowed to change position in the course of a round. A good sitting position will allow you to sit for a round of meditation without stress or strain, and also to stay awake. You can get advice about posture, but ultimately everyone has to experiment and find the postures that work best. In the course of a day of retreat, there are about twelve twenty-five-minute meditation periods, followed by five-minute periods of walking meditation. This you can do in the meditation hall or outside. After three or four rounds, there are longer breaks for mealtimes, rest periods or maybe to go for a walk.

Retreat participants are offered the greatest possible freedom. Apart from the general requirement to respect the silence and disturbing others as little as possible, your days are open to do as you please. Everyone decides for himself or herself if they want to sit for a round or take part in other activities, of which I will say more in a moment. I attach particular importance to people paying careful attention to how they feel, so that they can choose when to rest, move about or take part in rounds of meditation.

The silent sitting is important, but we also ask people to take care outside of the timed rounds of sitting, during meals for example. Meditation can be present during mealtimes when one is aware of much one is eating, and how quickly, and how the food tastes. Going to a retreat doesn't mean you have to give things up or become an ascetic; quite the contrary. It means that you try to experience and enjoy the little things, like a meal or going for a walk in a meditative manner.

Even when participants don't plan to do much in the retreat, there are various activities that take place every day. I give a talk every morning, there is group dialogue in the afternoon, and I also offer private meetings. Everything is optional. If you want to stay in silence and not say a word all week, you of course may do so. What does one do during the long periods of sitting meditation and the rest of the time, in a whole week of silent retreat? The answer is quite simple: listen, be aware. It is a matter of staying in the here and now, an inner state Toni Packer has called "awareness".

Nothing is excluded, as we become aware of all that reveals itself from one moment to the next. There is no goal. With these words we are saying everything and we are saying nothing at all, because meditation is something you experience. You live it. Talking about meditation can be interesting, exciting even; however, if you do not do it, if you do not actually practice meditation and set time aside for it, with some intensity, as in timed rounds of sitting, then it just becomes another subject of intellectual interest.

No one who doesn't have direct experience of how a seven-day retreat takes place can adequately describe these most simple of inner and outer forms. And no one has ever told me after their first retreat that it went exactly as they thought it would. In the final analysis, anyone really interested in meditation has to experience it directly and just go ahead and do it. How you meditate is not some kind of inaccessible mystery. It is perfectly possible to describe the essence of meditation in words, in speech or texts, which is what I have set out to do in this book. I should like people to approach meditation with something akin to playfulness. Feel free to experiment. Is it possible to enter into meditation as you read or as you raise your eyes from the page? What's it like for you? Anyone can become aware of what is going on within and experience awareness in the here and now, for however briefly.

In such a moment you are present, and aware of your bodily sensations. You can observe the thoughts and feelings that arise even as you read these words. When we allow ourselves a brief pause, as when we read, then we make more such moments possible: then you are meditating as you read, as I see it.

Toni Packer's books and talks foster this way of meditating. I shall say more about this in the last chapter of the book. When I read her words, a meditative mood asserts itself at once. This does not happen just to me. People often tell me that her words moved them to meditate, and that they want to seriously engage in the work.

My talks will speak for themselves. There are seven in all, from a seven-day retreat that took place in 2016. The texts are the edited recordings of these talks. I chose this form for the book because I didn't want to talk about meditation and all that it entails in a theoretical manner. I wanted to use the very words that came out of the stillness and silence of meditation. My words are alive with the spirit of meditation and do not come from theorizing, and it is my hope and wish that the book will be read in a meditative manner. I am inviting you to meditate with me. Nor am I first and foremost trying to communicate information, rather I am speaking directly to that intuitive and affective understanding that is a wondrous gift we all possess. Even though the verb "to understand" usually is associated with intellectual understanding; true human understanding merges into feeling, so the book speaks especially about the feeling associated with what is being described.

If this book gives you, the reader, some idea of what the stillness and silence of meditation can contribute to your life, or if it encourages you to meditate, then I will have achieved my purpose.

The First Evening

02 October 2016

The first time you come to a new place or, as is the case for many participants, you come to retreat after a year away, then we have what we call "orientation". Even when we know the place and recognize the people, everything is new like the first time. And for new people, the rules are all new and they don't know most of the other people in the retreat. There is a feeling of strangeness and alertness. Some people might find this stressful or even unpleasant, but the senses become focused and alert. All the senses become sharper and this makes it easier to see this with fresh eyes.

Asking "What's going on here?" is a good place to start. With this first moment of attentiveness, we can at once go further and ask: "What am I doing here? Why do I want to spend a whole week in silence?" Good questions. Why indeed do I want to sit in silence and meditate with everyone else here? What thoughts go through my mind when I ask these questions? Can you see for yourself what is going on within? What thoughts are going through your mind in this very moment? Are there images, desires? Are we seeking to attain something? Maybe we're trying to get rid of something. Maybe we're looking for peace and quiet because there's been a lot of stress and unrest in our life of late. And then we picture how we will quiet down here in retreat and how soon we'll be feeling better. We remember times in our lives when things were happier and more harmonious and we'd like to go back to those times.

Is it not astonishing how we are always taken up with expectations, desires and imaginings, whether we are here for the first time or for the tenth time? We always imagine what it will be like, and then almost always realize afterwards that it was different from what we had thought.

What does this work consist of? Can we start afresh? Can we look at all these ideas and images that flow through the mind with fresh eyes? Do we answer the questions that come up right away? Do we judge? "Yeah, it's going to work... no, this will never work ... ". Is it possible to listen to all the inner turmoil as for the first time and start anew, in the moment, in the Here and Now? Everyone can do this, at least for a moment.

What are we doing here? What's so special about a week of silence? The most important thing for me is the space and the free time. You can be with others and be alone, at one and the same time. You aren't alone in the sense of being lonely. Feeling lonely is something else again: you long for company. But here in retreat you're with others and at the same time you're on your own. Free of distractions, we can linger in the moment and see for ourselves what is taking place. Everything we have brought about in organizing the retreat – the silence, being with others but without speaking, a quiet room of one's own, plenty of space, and we can go for walks out in nature, good food we don't have to prepare – all these things come together to create a free and open space that invites us to become more aware of what happens in the moment. We have the time and the space in which to do this.

Do we like all this free time and space? There's nothing stopping you from asking. We can also choose to become closed in ourselves and narrow our outlook. You can look at this for yourself: Do you feel free? Are we respecting other people's space? We're not a group of individuals who have come together in retreat just to be alone; rather, we are a community. All of us either create a quiet open friendly space where we can all come together, or we can all get on one another's nerves in spite of the silence and go about shutting the door in someone's face and not paying attention as we go about our day. Can we see, from moment to moment, how we behave towards others? Is there really a shared, common attentiveness here in the retreat? This is something you can become aware of.

There is no need to feel cut off from others just because we don't say things like "Hi! - Good morning! - See you later!" to one another. We are all here together, and we can experience a warm sense of community that is even stronger than our everyday togetherness, with its little ritual greetings and courtesies. See for yourself if you can experience this simple, quiet and attentive way of being with others. Look to see if this is happening and if you can bring something to it.

If you have a roommate, can you feel the presence of the person you're sharing a room with? Are you aware of what your roommate likes and doesn't like? Do you leave the light on when there is no need, and dig about in plastic bags, unaware of how noisy that can be? Or are we just being present with those around us? You're resting, or your roommate is resting, and you both move about quietly. It's just a matter of being attentive and aware when you're around others. We don't make eye contact or smile as we pass one another. Still, we're all here together. Can we feel that it is OK to be around others without making eye contact? Try it and see how it goes. See for yourself if you feel it is being impolite not to make eye contact with others. What thoughts go through your mind? When someone keeps their eyes down, maybe we think they're depressed or just out of it. These are just images we have of others that most of the time have nothing to do with how they really are. Can we not say hello with the eyes as we pass someone and nonetheless feel that we are all here together? Can we give one another the space? This is a fine and free way of being together. When people come together in a group, this way of behaving is exactly what makes it possible for one to look inward without distractions and, in a spirit of inquiry, ask what is taking place from one moment to the next.

This is what we are doing here in retreat. You don't have to withdraw into your own private space. We just set aside our usual ways of reacting to others, our usual ways of behaving; that's all. We are simply here together; there are no requirements. Can we accept this attitude and even come to enjoy this way of relating to others? When we're lost in thought, the stillness and calm don't come about because we're so taken up by all the turmoil within. Here in retreat, we can just be aware of the inner turmoil, with no one to prevent us from observing what is going on within. No one is making any demands on you. We are free to inquire whether what is going on within is pleasant or unpleasant.

People often ask me if I can recommend a practice that can help to quiet down the mind and stop the endless flow of thought. We are each free to look within, to see what is taking place in the moment; but I don't consider this a practice. It's wonderful when there is a moment of stillness and silence, but it is not the purpose of meditation to make it happen. It isn't a matter of pursuing a goal, but rather of realizing that we are pursuing a goal. We have to see the importance of stillness and quieting down, without getting stuck in trying to get there. Indeed, observing our own striving, in order to better understand what is going on, is an essential part of this way of meditating. Often, we are not even aware that we are trying to get somewhere, that we are trying to reach a goal.

Since having goals is the very opposite of being attentive, I don't set goals for people, nor do I recommend meditative practices or exercises that can be used to reach a goal. Neither a special way of following the breath nor exercises in concentration are on the menu, which does not at all mean that I reject such practices out of hand. I know from personal experience how very useful such practices can be in helping one to be more focused; and sometimes, out of that a state of open awareness might unfold. If any of you have used these techniques in meditation and have found that they work well, you can use them here in this retreat; and if you want to share your experiences with others or if you have any questions, please bring them up with me or in group dialogue. "Practice" is a key term in the work of meditation.

You are free to choose how, and how much, you take part in the daily retreat schedule. Nothing is compulsory. You're free to choose those activities you find most helpful. There are more than ten rounds of meditation in a day, but you don't have to sit every round. Maybe you find it more appropriate to rest or go for a walk. Can we be attentive to the moment and observe what feels right, and take good care of ourselves? Nothing is compulsory. Quite the opposite: it's perfectly OK to skip a round or not go to a talk. But it is more than just OK. It's not as though we're putting up with it, rather it is in the very spirit of the retreat. No one is keeping count to see if you are sitting enough rounds or watching to see if you're doing everything the right way, nor do we prescribe a particular sitting posture. But if you have a question about posture, you can bring it up in a private meeting or in group dialogue, or write me a note.

It's important to me that you can sit in meditation without pain or strain. This is not a marathon. Rather we want to devote as much time as possible to being present and aware.

In the afternoon we set aside an hour for exercising in the meditation hall; and this week, one of the retreat participants happens to be a yoga teacher. She'll be leading a yoga session for those who are interested. Exercising is also optional, but I must stress how important it is to remain physically active in the course of a week that is given over to seated meditation. Our bodies need both moving and not moving, activity and stillness. The dynamic of change, from activity to stillness, is important for both our physical and spiritual well-being. See for yourself how much physical activity you need. Sometimes, after hours of sitting, a kind of dullness sets in, and you feel listless and sluggish. That's when physical activity can help, and not just yoga – you can go for a walk or go jogging or for a bike ride. But don't do it out of habit. I have seen for myself how sitting motionlessly, round after round, can make you feel wide awake, clear-headed and full of energy. Try to see what you need from one moment to the next.

And what about the talks? In this retreat we're even recording them, so don't be put off by the camera. We just want to make them available to people who can't come to retreat and to give you a chance to listen to them again, if you like.

I'm not trying to convince you of anything or to expound a teaching. Rather I speak of questions that come up for many people who engage in the work of meditation. I always speak of things I myself have experienced and that I want to share with you. Often, I tackle the themes and questions that have arisen for me in my own meditation work. Questions arise from the stillness, and in a talk, I try to express them in words. I ask questions, listen carefully to what comes out of the stillness and the silence, and then I speak. A talk does not express concepts and opinions, but rather lived experience and moments of insight that come up in the course of the talk and then find expression in words.

You have a chance to express yourself; not during the talk of course, but in one-on-one meetings with me or in group dialogue in the afternoon. Your feedback is most helpful. Can you not take the words I say too much to heart? Words are not the truth: all they can do is point to the truth. Now what I say may not be right or understood or complete. Please don't just believe what I say. Instead of just believing or not believing, can you look and listen carefully and come to know what is there behind the words? Instead of taking a stance that prevents you from listening to the next sentence, can you listen to your own feelings and reactions? Not hanging onto my every word, but rather go with the flow? You will have time later to look at what was said and make up your mind. That's what the talks are there for. And if I don't get my point across and something doesn't sit right with you, then please say so. I like it when people do that.

We can always look at a question again together with fresh eyes and find better words, words that work for both of us. There are as many ways of saying things as there are people to say them. Two people can have pretty much the same experience but will use different words to describe their experience and can interpret it differently. Words can be tricky. We often don't understand how they are being used, nor do we always remember exactly what was said.

And if we repeat their own words back to someone, it often comes out very different from what was actually said. Can we just see how what we say and write is always incomplete and so not take what is said too much to heart; and realize that words, written and spoken, are just a way for us to talk to one another? What is said can always be improved upon because it's not the words that matter but our shared understanding of things; is it not so?

The questions I discuss in my talks are not cut and dry, and for that reason they can always be gone into with different words and examples. The simplest and clearest way to say it is this: talks are there to awaken your interest in those questions that interest us all. We breathe life into the questions that interest us, so that we can look at them together with an alert and focused mind. Sometimes we find that a question we have been dragging around for the longest time has suddenly become clearer.

In every seven-day retreat, we clear up misunderstandings together. When, for example, we discuss questions brought up in a talk or by someone in group dialogue, we always discover new and different points of view; and there is always the possibility of all of us reaching a new understanding. That is what is so exciting about a week-long retreat: we can look deeply into the questions that come up. We have the time. There are no right or wrong answers; and when we look at a question with fresh eyes, new relationships can appear and be better understood.

There is awareness when we listen to one another, attentively, with focus. There is then a gathering of energy that makes it possible for us to go deeply into questions that interest us all, which is not possible when we are working on our own.

It is the purpose of a meditation retreat to go deeply into these questions and see for ourselves, through working with others, what is taking place in our lives from one moment to the next. Can we look deeply within, and seek an understanding that goes beyond the intellect and the thinking mind? Who are we really? Is there something to be seen and understood in the silence that cannot be put into words? Can we talk about these experiences with one another nonetheless, and find words that point the way? Let's leave the question open and answer-less. We can always look and see. . .

Questions of particular interest to you that don't go over well in a group can always be brought up in private meetings with me. You can bring up anything you want. I always listen with interest to your words. When we abandon all the conventional images that keep us apart, like "I'm the one leading this retreat and you're the student", then we can talk to each other openly and freely. You don't have to come in with a good question or bring up a particular aspect of the work of meditation. I have no such expectation. Two people meet on the same level and speak to each other in the moment. Maybe something will come up, maybe not – little matter. We sit quietly together and listen to the moment. Maybe a question will come up and we will both look at it, you with your energy and I with mine. Together we have twice as much energy. When two people come together like this in the stillness and silence of retreat to speak and to listen to each other, it is a kind of coming together that does not often take place in our everyday lives. This kind of exchange is never one-sided. I learn a great deal every time I meet someone in this manner. These private meetings are not just something that has to be done: you are all warmly invited to come talk with me.

When things are not going well or some problem comes up, I am available to talk with you anytime, and not just when time is set aside for one-on-one meetings. We can always meet someplace quiet where we can talk without disturbing others. Please don't expect too much of me: I don't have all the answers. But I have seen how talking about a matter without providing an answer can help throw light on a question by allowing you to step back from it. And I am not the only person you can discuss a problem with: when you are here in retreat with your spouse or trusted friend, you can go for a walk together and talk without bothering anyone. Or you can come in and talk with me two at a time.

Sometimes I address a question that has come up in a private meeting, in which case I will of course respect your privacy and not mention your name. Sometimes I can bring up your question using different words or in a different context. This doesn't mean that I have misunderstood. I may well have understood what you said but chose to tackle the question differently in the context of a talk. Whenever you feel you have been misunderstood or mis-quoted, please let me know.

Whether you come to meetings or not depends of course entirely on you, but please remember that meetings are very important to me. Without them, there is no group dynamic and everyone is on his own. If I were to be talking just for myself, without your feedback, then the talks would be lacking substance. When you have something to share, either in group dialogue or with me privately, then the greater part of what you say comes across to everyone in the retreat. This gives rise to a flow and a more intense exchange, and my talks become part of this flow. Of course, the same questions tend to come up in every retreat, but there is one thing I have noticed: what I say about the questions that come up depends upon what I hear from you. Only with your participation is there a heartfelt conversation, and are my talks then relevant and to the point.

That's enough talking. Have you noticed? It just started to rain. When we listen to a talk, we are often unaware of other sounds. When we concentrate on something, we filter out the present moment. Let's just listen to the rain and be with the moment.

Rainclouds above the fields – Schlagsuelsdorf
(Photograph by Rainer Simmelbauer)

Day 1: What is Meditation?

03 October 2016

What is meditation? The word summons up a host of associations. When we hear the word, we see people from different cultures and backgrounds engaged in Christian contemplation, or Buddhist meditation, doing Zen, or perhaps following Tibetan traditions. So many images come up from what we've heard or from what people have said, depending also on what we do ourselves or what we have learned. Maybe I say "my meditation" because I've worked out my own style. Is it possible to get closer to what meditation is, beyond words, concepts, systems and schools of meditation? Is there some element or essence that is common to all schools of meditation? I don't know if there is; but if it does exist, then we must be able to experience it in this very moment, right now. If you truly wish to find out what meditation is, then you must pay attention. There must be a listening. This listening, this paying attention with all the senses wide open – is this opening up of the self not the very mystery we seek to penetrate, beyond all practices and schools?

As we sit here together, in this quiet circle, just listening to the sounds around us, what is here? There is the sunlight streaming in through the windows onto the floorboards. Through the open window we can hear the chirping of a sparrow. But already that is saying too much: I said "floorboards" and "sparrow", and these words are language and present mental concepts, do they not? How can I go about describing what I see and what I am aware of in the moment? That which is being described is there, but there are no concepts. And what is it that cannot be expressed, when we don't think it through or put it into words? Can we ask the question and wonder in stillness? What is there right in front of us, from one moment to the next, if we do not give it a name? And who are we when we are just aware? This is where concepts cannot help us. The simple awareness of what is there in the moment, beyond all concepts, is, I am convinced, the very essence of meditation.

There is no need to describe in words what you see and hear and feel. The moment is a gift. It is there, just as it is. In the stillness of awareness, it is possible to go deeper into the moment, to open up more, to understand more and become even more aware. Awareness is not a superficial thing. Some event stands out from the flow of all that is happening and arouses our interest, gets our attention. This happens in a fraction of a second; and at once we try to classify it, we try to do something with it, to make sense of it. We at once describe to ourselves what has happened in order to see if it is good or bad. This emotional reaction is built-in; and if you think about it for a moment, you will see that it is a deep-rooted habit. A kind of judging takes place – "Is this a threat, or can I cope"?

The possibility of danger gives rise to worry and fear; but when it's something nice, the desire to possess, to acquire, is at once aroused. And with the desire to possess, images swim up – pictures and whole films, and often an inner monologue. All of this happens on its own, not through an effort of will; and in awareness it is seen at a glance.

It is really hard to simply become aware of our automatic reflexes and stay aware in the present moment. The sheer number and multiplicity of inner happenings easily takes us away from looking and seeing and just becoming aware – instead, the brain falls into the well-worn rut of familiar programs: this is the tried and true way the body reacts to being overwhelmed with information. Often, we find ourselves looking at the moving picture show within, without noticing where we actually are. The here and now has given way to remembering, and these memories we take for reality. To wake up from this inner picture show and find ourselves once again in the here and now – this is the essential element in our meditation work. To be aware of what's happening in the here and now, to see memories for what they are, one memory surging up after another – this is the work of meditation.

There is no specific technique or practice to help you become aware, or to help bring awareness about. Awareness comes about on its own, always. There is a moment of awakening, the sudden awareness that you have stopped dreaming and see that, in reality, you are sitting there meditating. Awareness is our astonishment and amazement at what is unfolding right in front of our eyes, from one moment to the next. Do you have the interest to do this work? Do you feel that it is within your grasp?

To be honest, we often don't want to be in touch with what is there because the present moment is not always very pretty. Perhaps there is an inner discomfort, a stream of images and thoughts from yesterday at work that we would like to drop but just cannot. This all takes place in the moment and we can perceive it with interest; but then resistance arises and then judgement: "No, I don't want this, it should stop! I don't want to fret and worry about a job waiting for me at work!"

Can we pause, in the very midst of all this wanting and not wanting? We don't really make this happen, and that's what is so lovely about it: it happens all on its own, unbidden. All of a sudden, we wake up: "I'm sitting here in the meditation hall, I'm not at work or in the situation I thought I was in." Is it possible to stay in the here and now, whatever may come up? What is there here, in this very moment? The torrent of thoughts and images flowing through us with their attendant feelings and emotions ceases all on its own, and we find ourselves in the stillness of the meditation hall, sitting quietly together with others. We feel our bodily sensations, maybe a bit of excitement from what we've been thinking about.

Can we just be present with the bodily sensations, with breathing in and breathing out? Breathing in and breathing out is always there, for as long as we live. Breathing is the anchor that keeps us in the moment. When we become aware of our breathing, we see at once that a moment before we were not aware - other sensations were there in its place. Being aware means just being with what is from one moment to the next. It does not exclude anything, not even the torrent of thought flowing through the mind. Do we have to bring thinking under control? Not at all. It means just being aware that the thoughts and feelings and images are just what they are, thoughts and feelings and images that arise, in the moment. Is this possible?

We can distinguish between two ways of thinking. Thoughts can arise on their own and run automatically, like a film on a screen in our head. We are caught up in the dreaming, in the film that is always orchestrated by the feelings and emotions that feed the narration and just go on and on. We identify with this stream of thought, which means that we are unaware that the torrent of thought and feeling comes from within, and we often speak and act as though the inner film were real, and the body follows suit.

The anger and anxiety that comes up is real, and in the moment. Since everything feels real and there is also a physical, bodily reaction, we identify with this inner narrative. We say: "This is what I am, right in this moment", even when the story playing within is just memories from ten years before.

But you may also be aware that you are thinking. Then there is a subtle inner difference: we become aware that these thoughts and feelings are running through our mind all on their own, in this very body, as I sit here quietly. But we are seldom aware in this manner and we stay trapped and caught up in our usual ruts of feelings and thoughts.

Awareness needs space. Most of the time we go through our everyday lives filled up to the brim with thoughts and feelings that take up all of the inner space, so that it looks like there is no room for the present moment. There is no room left to see that thoughts are just thoughts, and to be clearly aware that feelings are coursing through the body. We live in a state of unawareness. Our over-loaded body-mind switches to automatic in order to cope with life, and this by and large is a useful function that helps us survive in situations where we feel overwhelmed.

Many schools of meditation try to control this flood of thought with various concentration practices and these practices have their place and can work – this must be said. But I must admit that I am not very good at using concentration to control my thoughts. One thing is clear: when thoughts and feelings so overwhelm us that we just can't see what is taking place, then it can indeed be helpful to start out with a concentration practice.

I lead a meditation group that meets every Tuesday. Once, a man who had never meditated before joined us. After the rounds of meditation, he told me how it had gone. The three twenty-five minute rounds of meditation had stressed him out so much and caused him such unease that he automatically started to count. He counted slowly up to sixty, at which point he knew another five minutes had passed in the round. He repeated counting until he was saved by the bell. He told us that this had helped him get through the three rounds. I was astonished. Without any instruction, he had found a concentration practice all on his own. Counting in this manner, with awareness, helps one to focus and break the automatic flow of thought, at least for as long as one counts in an attentive manner.

It is a good learning experience to give such practices a try for yourself, even if I don't directly recommend it. It throws light on the matter, to ask oneself how a concentration practice, like counting or the recitation of a mantra, or focusing on your breathing or on a part of the body, can help us see the effects of such a practice on the body-mind. In speaking with people, I hear time and again how very difficult it is to even begin to become aware of what is taking place from one moment to the next. People often ask me if I can suggest a practice, if it would be easier to start sitting with a practice of some kind. Here, in retreat, you have the time to give it a try. There is no right or wrong when there is genuine interest in seeing and understanding.

My own experiments with concentration practices allowed me to see the usefulness and shortcomings of such practices. To concentrate means that we set ourselves a goal to which we cling with tenacity. If I have as my goal to carefully observe my breathing, an interesting duality presents itself: first there is me, and then there is the goal I am pursuing. I'm in control for as long as I'm doing it right and I'm aware that I have a job to do. Am I following my breath, or have I already gone off on a tangent? Someone is in control and keeps an eye on things and is busy concentrating as best they can; and then there is the concentration on the breathing, which is separate and apart. Following the breath is what we are supposed to be doing. But then images come up, and without wanting to, we lose our focus and find ourselves back where we started, lost in thought, and we think. . . "I wanted to stay with my breathing. . .". Can you see the duality? Does there have to be someone there who has to be in control doing the concentrating, and judging whether or not we are doing it right? Is there not simply awareness of the breathing in the midst of everything that swims up into consciousness? Must there be someone who is aware, someone who keeps an eye on whether we are aware or not? Not at all, because when this "controller" steps in, and we are looking carefully, we might see that there is no one there doing the controlling but simply controlling thoughts that have arisen. See for yourself if this is so.

With concentration practices, we are for the most part unaware of the effort to control: we just don't see that in truth there is no such entity like a controller. Our narrow focus has to widen, and if this happens concentration turns into awareness. The effort of concentration gives way to an effortless awareness that requires no doer or controller, and the breath flows in and out all on its own. People who like working with concentration practices and who have used them a lot have told me that when it works, when the practice is going well, they experience what I have here called "a turn into awareness". The controlling ceases.

Where are we really, when there is just moment-to-moment awareness? Where is the man called "Stephan"? Who is it that is being aware? Or is it that no one is there? My question means: is it possible to be aware, to be wholly present, without a state of duality that says – "I am someone experiencing awareness"? Can all that I perceive as my thoughts and feelings and goals simply become part of the undivided whole? Can we simply recognize all this without identifying with it, without even giving any of it a name? In truth, we do not know who we really are. We have thoughts about who we are, or images and pictures of who we are; but in awareness these representations are seen for what they are, just representations; which means they can be questioned and looked into and seen for what they are – thoughts and images. This can only take place when we do not identify with them. Can we take a step back and clearly see that what we take to be the self and our personality is made up of thoughts and feelings? When we do not know who we are and just see with the inner eye, then we come closer to what we really are.

Meditation practices that use concentration are out there. They present the self as an actor on stage, but it's entirely possible for the concentrating self to come into awareness. Then there remains just awareness and no one who is aware – no one doing anything, no one engaged in a meditation practice, which means there is no practice in the usual sense of the word. This is what I mean when I say that this kind of meditating, in which there is just awareness, is not really a practice.

In many schools of meditation, the word "mindfulness" is much used, and sometimes it's given the same meaning as "awareness"; but for me the two words are not synonymous. In the word "mindfulness", I always see the attentive observer, an "I", someone who is there. What is there, what happens when the person being mindful becomes the very object of the mindfulness, when the person being mindful is seen to be just another image? What is it that is so carefully observing the mindful one? There's no one there. Is it not so? Awareness can then throw light on the one who is being mindful. Try this for yourself. Awareness can come into being, but it's hard to put into words because in awareness no one is present: the one who is aware dissolves in the light of awareness. A living awareness unfolds from one moment to the next, and at the same time no one is present – there is just the wordlessness of not knowing. Understanding comprises knowing and naming and judging; but simple awareness is a kind of knowing that cannot be communicated to another: it is simple and spontaneous and one with all that is taking place in the moment. When the creation of images comes to a complete standstill, there is neither big nor small, neither wide nor narrow.

Is it therefore possible for us, in the course of the week, perhaps when the merry-go-round of thought slows down, to bring this attentiveness and concentration and practice over into our work of insight, so that we are no longer hemmed in and focused? Is this possible? Do we have to be in control? Do we have to actively drop all thoughts? Do we have to strain and strive?

When there is effort, can we simply see it happening? Effort is in the body, and it can be felt in the tensing of the muscles. There is the feeling that a strong effort of will is necessary in order to stay on course and reach our goal. How about when effort is seen as what it is instead of being used as a tool for intensely looking inward? How about when bodily tension comes to consciousness, when we become aware of the strain and effort, when our striving to reach a goal comes into the light of awareness? Is there perhaps a new gateway opening for us?

Is it then possible to arrive at a deeper understanding of this astonishing living body-mind? Often, straining and striving just drop away when they come into awareness. When we become aware of tensions in the body, stiffness in the shoulders for example, what exactly takes place? Almost at once we let our shoulders drop and relax. Maybe you have already experienced this, and felt them tighten up again after a short while. Usually this is when awareness has not lasted. After a fleeting glance at what is taking place, we find ourselves back in the state of duality and back to striving and controlling. We can get used to straining and striving, so that we're hardly aware of it any more. But even a brief and momentary awareness of the straining and striving to reach a goal is not without meaning. When something has been seen, it's like a seed, and it can happen again. The possibility of awareness is part of the make-up of this astounding body-mind, and the beauty of awakening is that it happens all on its own. Awakening is spontaneous and does not come about by effort of will, and it happens again and again. Can you observe all of this for yourself?

For example, as we are sitting here, old memories come up. We get lost in remembering, and then suddenly we wake up and see where we are and think: "I'm just sitting here, and those are just old memories coming up, that's all it is."

Can we simply savor this moment of awareness and just appreciate it for what it is? Maybe we became aware of something that makes us uncomfortable. In spite of this, the moment of awareness offers us the possibility of staying aware for a while longer. We are waking up and we look around us. I cannot say it without duality as I have to use words. But this is just waking up. It does not consist of saying, "I'm waking up." This moment of awareness quite literally reveals reality - not what I would like it to be, but what is really there. Can we simply see what is taking place and stay with it? That's enough. What we see may not be very important, but the fact that we have been given a glance at reality, directly, is that not meaningful in itself? No one did this. We simply woke up. This is what is so marvelous about awareness.

Is it not enough to just be there and not do anything, but just stay with it when a moment of awareness manifests? But what can we do when questions persist and our problems will not give us any peace? Does it help to look for answers when existential questions and our needs overwhelm us? "What's going to happen to me when I get old? Is there anything after death?" – Questions like this can torture us. Can we just let these answer-less questions be? Can we simply concentrate on our breath and breathe them away? Maybe we can approach them in a meditative way, these existential questions, since our usual way of tackling them doesn't work.

A question like, "Where is Luebeck?" is easy to answer: just walk up the hill and you can see the towers of Luebeck in the distance. We can even answer such a question without speaking, and just point to the towers of the town. But existential questions are different in nature because they do not have concrete answers. We don't know what it means to no longer "be". All of our experiences are life experiences. Even death we only know through others, and "not being" lies completely outside our understanding. Are these questions therefore meaningless, as we often hear? Hearing this is of no use when the questions are of burning importance to us.

How can we go about approaching these existential questions? Can we just be with them, in stillness and silence? Is it possible to leave them there in the silence, and just listen? When there is no answer, there is the space for something to reveal itself. It's not a matter of engaging in discursive thought; it's enough just to ask your question into the silence and let it be. You can ask without knowing the answer or probing any deeper: "What does it mean, to die?" – you can ask the question, and in stillness, open yourself to the silence. Let go of ideas and images, and your fears also. . . This perhaps is what we are really seeking: to go on existing, in perpetual contradiction to our longing for peace. We are full of contradictions. Can we let it all be, and allow the spectacle of thoughts and feelings to just fade away, without hoping for results? Inner clarity can simply mean that we suddenly understand why the question will not leave us in peace. I've already experienced how a question can just dissipate, leaving no answer, when all the fears and images connected with the question come into the light of the present moment and lose all meaning and thus breaking their hold over us.

Meditative inquiry is a way of silently questioning and listening, and sometimes a hidden inner process comes into awareness. Conventional thinking with questions and answers offers nothing new, and conventional answers are stored away in memory and summoned up at will. Asking a question in a meditative manner is, on the contrary, a creative process. Can we ask a question and consciously abstain from seeking an answer, and just listen to how this body-mind reacts, and see the thoughts and feelings and images that surge up into awareness? Can we observe the answers that come up without believing them and holding onto them? Can everything, including these feelings that come up here and now in the meditation hall, be looked at as for the first time, with that open inner space that leaves room for the chirping of the sparrows outside? (Sparrows are chirping outside.)

So how does it work? How can one just be with a question? And how can a whole question perhaps just cease, here in the stillness? This happens. See for yourself. At such a time, there are just the bodily sensations, the breathing, here and now, in the moment. What we see and hear is all there, present from one moment to the next. There is nothing that has to be done, nothing that has to change. When the driving need to get something or to understand something has abated and we are at one with the moment, no me-person exists and there is nothing to be understood. Where is the question at such a moment? Where are the problems? Everything is as it is and we are just here in the stillness and awareness.

Are we here?

Luebeck- View from the hills behind the village of Schlagsuelsdorf
(Photograph by Walter Rapf)

Day 2: Feelings

04 October 2016

"Think before you act!" These words from my childhood still resonate with me and often come to mind. That's what my father always said to us kids, mostly when something got broken because of our rambunctious running about. But what does it really mean? The words seem to say that we think first and that actions stem from the thoughts, or that that's the way it should be. But is this really the way our actions come about? In Western culture we have foremost in our minds the conviction that we are rational beings who think and then act, and that this is what makes us human. But if our actions do not arise from thinking, then where do they come from? Is it possible to set aside opinions and thoughts and convictions and look within, directly, from moment to moment, to see where our actions come from? We can do this together right now. Maybe we'll discover that seeing our convictions in a rational manner is just another idea in itself. What is it really like?

This morning, as I was walking through the park on my way to the pond, the question came up again: who's in the driver's seat? Who or what is it that sets the body in motion, that lets us walk and act? Instead of thinking about it, I just looked to see what was taking place. While I was walking along, a whole series of feelings and bodily sensations came up. An impulse pulled me along in that direction, so I walked up the hill and I saw the big rock and the bench and at once, all by itself, the thought appeared: "That's where I'm going!" But did the thought bring about the decision to go up to the bench? The decision preceded the thought, and the body was already moving and heading for the bench. The thought came after: action flowed from feeling and from the body moving; that could be seen. Is this so surprising? We always want to be rational and take the reins in hand and be in charge of our life; but when we're just walking along a path, it's our feelings and physical movements that take us in one direction or another.

There was no conflict, by which I mean no thoughts of "No". Thinking came along for the ride, so to speak, accompanying an action that had already been decided upon and was in full swing.

But we often experience the conflict between thought and feeling, in that we think that we want one thing and the body does not go along with it or does something else. In my experience, at such times, feelings win out over thought.

I have an old memory to share with you. I was sixteen years old and on a class outing. In the youth hostel where we were staying there were students in our age group from all over Germany. I found a girl from another class very attractive. I clearly remember thinking, "This is your chance to talk to her." It was just the right moment: she was down in the yard sitting by herself reading. I was right near-by and no one else was around. The thought was: "Get down there and talk to her!", but I hesitated and felt blocked and my feet wouldn't move. The thinking mind was saying: "What could go wrong?", but that didn't help any. I stood rooted to the spot for at least two long minutes and then my big chance was gone: she got up and went into the house.

I can still remember the deep frustration that rose up within. I felt dumb and inadequate. Thoughts kept running around in my head: "Why didn't you go over and introduce yourself? Other guys do it!". A wave of shame and anger and disappointment swept over me; and when I look back and remember that day, the very same feelings rise up. I feel the same fear of rejection. It was the strongest feeling of all, and now I understand what was happening: it was the fear that brought about the decision not to act. But what was the source of the acting or not acting that so confused me at the time? At the time I had not understood, and the self- doubt that came out of it pushed me into an inner crisis.

When we move in a certain direction, the whole body comes into play; and the body is alive with feelings and impulses. Thoughts that are present enter into this process, for thoughts release feelings. This can be seen directly, but often we ourselves don't know the meaning of our feelings.

How good are we at coming into contact with the flow of feelings and emotions within? Can we feel with the gut, which is where there can be direct awareness of what is taking place? Can we ask ourselves: "What are feelings and emotions anyway?" Is it possible to listen to them and see them as they manifest and make themselves known?

I have always found it useful in thinking things through to work with a theme, like the subject of today's talk. It tries to grasp the meaning of our feelings by looking at them from the scientific point of view, while remaining level-headed and detached and thus remaining open to learning something new. In this way it is no longer just about me and my problems, but about making observations that can be of use to anyone.

Why are we humans so emotional? Why do we have feelings in the first place? Feelings are ancient. Research into the workings of the brain revealed that emotions are present in primitive organisms like reptiles. If we are to believe the researchers, emotions and feelings first came into being some 350 million years ago, as the brain structures of the early reptiles (who are our ancestors) became more complex. Feelings and emotions were generated and developed; and, in their more evolved state, became part of the mental make-up of the species.

How even earlier forms of life behaved we shall leave aside, but with reptiles we can see what happened: they see their prey and then there is a complex emotional reaction. They don't seem to think, but there is an emotional reaction – they experience, things like repulsion and danger. They can be frightened and take flight, and can become angry and aggressive. They're not just robots responding to stimuli. The most basic emotions are clearly in place. Who is to say they don't experience anger and fear just like we do?

Greed was one of the first emotions to come into being. The early animals first and foremost needed to eat, and then to reproduce; which is to say they first craved food and then sexual partners. With humans, these feelings have become vastly more complex and broader in scope. The original desires are still there but we lust after nice cars, the latest fashions, are greedy for power and fame, and have an insatiable desire for recognition. Luckily, all of our greed for accomplishment and acquiring things can be seen directly.

Can you see that it is not simply a matter of having thoughts about wanting and desiring, and that there is a powerful physical drive behind it all? This is what it means to be human: we suffer physically if we don't get what we want. Our emotions have such power because our whole body is actively engaged. It also happens all on its own, like background music; that our needs dress themselves up as thoughts that play out as movies, whole feature films, in which we have already reached our goals and satisfied our desires.

A feeling is always a complete activation of the body that sits right here in the gut, something we can feel directly and intensely. Do we want to look? What is fear? Anger? Can we become directly aware that there is a tightening in the chest when we experience fear, for example? Are we interested in feeling that there is suddenly a knot of tension in the gut? There is a tightening of the muscles, there is no mystery there. When we experience fear, certain muscles tense up and other bodily functions almost shut down completely; the digestive system does this, for example, and then the stomach is stressed.

A further example: when I experience fear or get excited, my fingers often get cold: the blood vessels in the extremities contract. How does this happen? These are ancient reflexes, mechanisms that run all on their own, just as they functioned in the earliest primeval reptiles. Anger and fear alert the body to act so that we can be ready to fight or flee. They can still save your life. The digestive system does not receive more blood because the muscles need it to fight or flee. Blood flow to the hands and feet is reduced because the extremities are most likely to be injured and reducing the blood flow helps avoid loss of blood. Even the immune system gets ready to fight off germs that get in through open wounds. That feelings like fear (even though we don't want to experience them) are important for our survival, we can see very clearly when we remember past dangerous situations. Fear is a warning to us to run out of the way of on-coming traffic. This action is already under-way and makes us stop in our tracks before a single thought has time to arise.

I have vivid memories of one such instance: a car was com-ing right towards me, brakes squealing, and I just froze. I was lost in thought and just hadn't noticed the car. At first, I felt blocked and just stood there. Then I saw the car and saw how I was just standing there, and only then did I feel fear. And then the danger was past.

There are things that take place within us that precede thinking. The brain becomes active and initiates feelings of fear before we become aware of what is happening. The brain centers involved first appeared in animals that ap-parently lacked the structures required for the conscious processing of data. Only later in the evolutionary process did they come into being, when new brain structures evolved like the cerebral cortex, which made possible complex thought and complex representation and gave rise to human awareness.

But the emotions continued to play a dominating role in our lives. They operate autonomously and help us sur-vive. Our awareness is activated when the body is already in motion and feelings are already holding sway. This is why we often feel that our feelings cannot be controlled.

I can give you an example of something we have all expe-rienced. Have you ever noticed what takes place when you get a scare? Let's say you're going for a walk after dark and suddenly someone taps you on the shoulder. You are at once gripped by fear and the whole body springs into action and is fully engaged before we become aware of what is happening; and only then do we start to think. We get our bearings and see what is taking place. We may have stepped away or even jumped to one side; then we see that a friend had snuck up behind us and was just playing a trick on us. The body immediately starts to relax but the fear and tension linger awhile.

Fear suddenly arises and goes away; we can see how the whole thing just takes place on its own. We are equipped with an emotional structure that does not allow us to choose to react: before we know it, we have reacted. The structure of feelings does not distinguish between a real threat or a memory. Only gradually do we perceive the difference. When memories are involved, the bodily reactions are not as strong because we are just reliving a traumatic experience.

We can learn here and now how our feelings operate in that we can see that our memories exist, not just as thoughts and images, but also in the realm of strongly-felt emotions.

When feelings arise, they alter our relationship to others and to the world around us. They can be a link to others and to the world around us or they can keep us apart. Have you ever noticed how feelings can separate people from one another? Fear, anger, disgust and also greed all have the effect of separating us from others. Why is this so? Fear, for example, brings with it the spontaneous realization that this entirely separate body is under threat and must be protected. This is only possible in a world where everything is divided up into that which poses a threat and that which must be protected. Any form of self-centered awareness signifies separation: this body, which I am, must be protected. I'm sitting here, I'm hungry, I need something.

This fundamental, underlying separate-ness arises and manifests endlessly in our thoughts. We separate everything into good and bad, into that which is desired and the person who desires. All duality is rooted in feelings that separate us from others – thoughts that separate pale in comparison to the intensity of feelings that keep us apart. Separation is all-powerful in the presence of fear. When we are frightened, our whole being becomes a lonely and helpless individual who needs help and protection.

But this is just one side of the coin. The other side has feelings like love, joy and achievement, which bring us closer to others. These feelings we also experience in the body and they are as real as the feelings that separate us from others. We always long for this extremely pleasant and intense physical bond. Feelings on bonding, of connectedness, tell us that we are one with the world: nothing can happen to us, no one is a stranger and all is well. We have all experienced such moments and want to experience them again; we want to lose ourselves in them. We want to become one with others in this state of joy; and when we are truly in love we don't want to feel as one with the beloved, but rather we feel as one with the whole world.

Can we, in our meditation, give feelings the full importance they have? Can we give our feelings the same attention we give to our thoughts? It's a matter of coming directly into contact with our feelings. The most astounding observations then become possible. When do we feel complete? Connected to others? At one with them? Fulfilled? Is it possible to put such a question in a meditative manner, and then see if this reveals anything?

Astonishingly, connectedness with others just appears when all the feelings of separation have quieted down, when anger and fear are not there, when we no longer worry about ourselves and our preferences or the future. When all that separates us from others falls away, when we're standing on solid ground, there is no separation. Look for yourself to see if what I'm saying is true!

Usually, we are far removed from this ground upon which thoughts and feelings come to rest. Often when we begin a week of meditation, we feel unsettled; and this feeling pulls us in all directions, not only to where we find ourselves. When things quiet down and there is some peace, we become aware of how many divisive thoughts flow through the body in a rush. And in all likelihood, it was the same on previous days; but our busy-ness just kept us from seeing. By busy-ness I mean feelings like, "I have to go here or there, I must accomplish something". This doesn't stop when you go to retreat.

Can we look at the source of this restlessness? What part of it may we observe directly? When the outside noise and excitement quiets down, we think we can just get back to our inner peace; but our inner ability to generate thoughts and images compensates for it with even greater unrest.

A reptile sunning itself is presumably at peace and at one with the world. That's how it appears to me when I observe the little snakes in the rock garden at Springwater. They're warm and their bellies are full and they're happy, until a new challenge comes up. We sit here; everything is taken care of, maybe you even slept well, and ideally there's nothing wrong at all. But we are nonetheless ill at ease and full of thoughts and more than anything else we just want to get away from here. Something is lacking and we just feel unconnected. Is that not astonishing? Can we just look carefully at this for a moment and see what is taking place from one moment to the next? What force is pulling at us? These are impulses, emotions, that the body has activated and that pull us in all directions. We are not imagining this; it is the truest meaning of the word 'reality'. This unrest is at work within us, here in this very body. It happens that thoughts and images release ever more emotions; and in turn allow ever more thoughts and images to arise. Our brains are so big and have stored away so much information that there are always memories and images and associations popping up.

Our network of emotions makes it seem that all this activity is coming from outside of us. We've all experienced how a simple thought can get us all worked up. "I forgot to turn off the gas", or "There was something important I wanted to tell people at work!" It's as though we're getting ready to break into a run. What can we make of all of this? Are we entirely helpless? Is there some way of keeping it in check, some way of observing it from moment to moment?

Feelings manifest in the body differently from thoughts. They come up but they don't go away as quickly as thoughts or images. When a feeling arises, it affects the organs and the muscles; and there follows a cascade of released molecules, hormones and mediator-chemicals, brought about by complex bodily reactions. This goes on until a feeling has subsided. Feelings affect us physiologically - for example, your stomach can be all in knots - and then the body slowly quiets down when nothing happens, when thinking quiets down, no more images come up and nothing changes in our surroundings. It lasts a few long minutes, not hours, and already the body is quietening down.

This is perhaps easiest to observe after some frightening thoughts that seem to be irrelevant and serving no purpose. The body has already received the message: "False alarm. You can just carry on." Depending on how great the fright was, our reaction to it might subside quickly or more slowly. But as long as thinking is still stimulated and old memories and frightening images surge up, the body does not quiet down.

Our huge store of associations almost always brings up something that presents itself as real life – a frightening memory brings with it feelings of fear. Memories of past anger elicits feelings of anger. For example, if we are feeling hard done by, we'll think that we are not getting what's due to us. Then all those situations come to mind in which we did not get what was coming to us and we felt cheated. What do we do now with all these thoughts and feelings? In a kind of hellish cycle, they give rise in turn to yet more strong feelings. Instead of there being a return to inner quiet and peace, more emotional excitement comes up. Nor can one just turn it off, for the thoughts and images come up spontaneously. We really don't know what exactly cause them. There is no one doing it; at least, I have never come upon the originator of thought.

Look for yourself: is there someone doing it? A memory comes up all on its own, and at once an emotion is released. And so our feelings go up and down and back and forth, and after a while the memory that caused all the fuss is forgotten; but then something else pops up. Is it possible to be steady and patient and behold what is taking place? Astonishingly, when there is awareness and we just stay with it and observe the coming and going of feeling and thought, it is like introducing sand into the gears of the whole process.

When we stay in the moment and observe how a memory or an image can arouse feelings in the body, and how the emotions then give rise to thoughts – when there is awareness of this process and a certain distance from it - then the whole thing just falls apart on its own. There would appear to be an intelligence within us that tells us when it is no longer necessary to go any further with thoughts and feelings. This occurs when it is perfectly clear that we are in the here and now and that there is no present danger: we see that this is just old stuff, memories that rise up out of our great store of things remembered.

We often confuse memory with reality. We don't recognize that we're just caught up in thought and memories, like in a film that is running all on its own. Sand gets into the works and then all at once we see that the film is just a film and that we're living in the here and now. We become aware that we are here in the present and that thoughts and feelings bring about the images. This waking up seems to be spontaneous. We have all experienced it at one time or another. It often brings with it a quieting down. Our whole body becomes still and quiet because the cause for the unrest has fallen away, and the body stops producing the hormones that stress us out.

Is it possible for us to align our feelings with the present moment, even when fear and anger rage within us? Can we reach the point where we experience the whole process in the moment, while it is perfectly clear that we are sitting on a chair here in the meditation hall? Sitting here is the reality in which thoughts and images and feelings appear.

You can see for yourself if this is possible and if things change, but don't expect too much too quickly: it is so very easy to lose your way again and then no longer be aware that you are sitting on this chair. But as long as there is awareness, a certain intelligence acts; the body is not over stimulated and new thoughts and images pass by as if they were clouds.

All the free time and the outer stillness and quiet allow us to become more sensitive. Old memories, often tied into powerful emotions, pile up. Things we have been repressing rise to the surface unbidden, and it is no easy thing to observe the roiling emotions, without reacting. Traumatic memories can swim into awareness and overwhelm us. The more intense they are the more space they take up, and the easier it is for these strong emotions to carry us away from the present moment.

Awareness is not a panacea we can use to overcome old traumas. It is not a psychological tool we can use to bring memories that have always tormented us up into the light, so that we see through and lay them to rest. Sometimes this is very clear and an inner voice tells us that this is not the moment to dive into an old trauma.. Can we hear this voice also? Can we simply stay there with that which reveals itself and not try to indulge in self-therapy? Often, seeing is knowing and change comes about quietly and undramatically; there is no one doing anything. However hurt we may be, we have the ability to heal within.

I remember how, in retreats over the years, I always had one really bad day: I would feel unwell and my whole life seemed just awful. I couldn't figure out what was going on. There was this lump in my stomach and I was worried about what was happening. Nothing ever came of it, and after a while I noticed that the knot in my stomach would just go away. But in the next retreat it would come back. Today, looking back, I realize that it has just gone away. Whatever it was, one thing is sure: everything is in flux. Nothing remains unchanged, even when we torment ourselves with the thought that it will never go away. In my case, whatever it was just went away, without drama, and I only noticed it in retrospect.

Can we give this endless stream of thoughts, images and imaginings, and the attendant symphony of feelings, the attention it deserves from one moment to the next? Can you do this without knowing, without judging or thinking about it, without having a goal? Can you just look and allow the whole thing to take place, as though we just want to study what is happening and not want to act? Mind you, to want to study oneself is already going too far. Is such a thing possible?

When we start out with the strong desire to become quieter and know again the state of stillness that we experienced once before, then we find ourselves in full wanting mode. Where there is wanting and a longing for something, there is also separateness and division. It amounts to saying: "I'm lacking something, I have to get something!" Just for a little while, can we not want anything, not want to get anywhere? Just see what is taking place in the here and now, within and without? That's what this work is all about, and we cannot say what will come out of it.

Things change, and we change also. When there is a real interest in wanting to know ourselves, when we observe what is happening within, then we are already meditating. The astonishing thing is that when presence manifests and abides a while, then all our mental and bodily processes quiet down all on their own and we suddenly find ourselves there, where we were longing to be. In inner stillness and silence, body and mind are at rest.

Can we come to see and understand how wanting and striving work against inner silence and stillness? They separate us from the flow of life; without wanting and striving we move effortlessly through the waters of life. When it becomes clear to us that there is nothing lacking, nothing that has to be done, when we are simply present with what is there in the moment, then inner stillness comes about all on its own, accompanied by feelings such as joy. Perhaps there will be a feeling of Oneness with others in this amazing world in which we find ourselves. When feelings that separate are no longer there, Oneness steps in and takes their place.

Schlagsuelsdorf Park
(Photograph by Stephan Bielfeldt)

Day 3: Ego Mind

05 October 2016

When you are still, and thoughts and feelings have quieted down, what else is there, really? Maybe you are just going for a walk, and the stillness comes into awareness. Then there is just walking, the sound of your steps, your breathing, the lovely red berries on the bushes, the sun breaks through the clouds and disappears again, the cold wind caresses your face. There is just this awareness, and there are no questions. There is nothing to explain, nothing is required, everything is already there, in fullness and emptiness.

Often, the stillness is there for only a moment; and then the thoughts return, and memories follow, one after the other, pictures in the mind. With the thinking comes feelings, desires, needs, fears. Experiencing the silence gives rise to a question: what is this simple state of being in which the "I" is absent? Is there some separate being, an "I" that exists at all? What exactly is taking place?

In the course of a week-long meditation retreat, it is good to look within and spend time with these questions. Who is this person we call, "I", and who are you? What are other people? What are we, from one moment to the next? Can we find clear answers to these questions, or are the answers we find just imaginings? Not only does the question of who we are come up time and again, but many thoughts of how we would like to be and what we would like to achieve in life also come up. We are ourselves at the center of most existential questions; and we ask these questions not only because we are interested, but also out of a feeling of distress. Who am I? Where did I come from? What will become of me?

Do we ask ourselves such questions in full awareness? Most of the time we do not. We may be aware that these questions and worries are already present, without consciously thinking about them. When they arise in our consciousness, it's like a puzzling problem that we suddenly become aware of.

Is it possible for us to ask these existential questions here and now, in a meditative manner? This means that we are not actively looking for answers, rather we just ask the question and then carefully look at what comes up.

The inquiry into our own being might become wider by including all human beings and all of nature.. A question on humanity came up to me recently and I'd like to share it with you. It was: "What are we humans, and what is it that makes us human? This spring I read an interesting article in a German edition of Scientific American [1] about the development of humankind over the last fifty thousand years or so. I was amazed. Back then, we were just a small group of so-called modern men living in a corner of southeast Africa. About sixty thousand years ago, our ancestors increased greatly in numbers; and, in an amazingly short period of time, spread out over the entire world.

Other species of humans had appeared before us - the Neanderthals in western and northern Europe, and Denisova humans in Asia; they had been around for tens of thou-

---

[1] Marean, C. W. (2015). The most invasive species of all. Scientific American, 313(2), 32-39.

sands of years already. Then our species came out of Africa and, in about thirty thousand years, settled the whole of Europe and Asia. Even the scientists researching this phenomena were stunned: How could this have taken place so quickly? And the settling of the Americas went even faster. About fourteen thousand years ago (during the last Ice Age), the sea-bottom was exposed and there was a land-bridge between Asia and North America, where there is now the Bering Strait. It took less than a thousand years for humankind to settle the whole of North and South America. Suddenly, in the archaeological record, we find traces of modern humans, all the way from Alaska to Tierra del Fuego. This sounds like a success story, but most success stories have a dark side. This wave of migration doomed the earlier species of man: about thirty thousand years ago, the Neanderthals died out in Europe, as did Denisova-humans in Asia.

It is still not clear exactly what happened. Did modern humans deprive them of their habitat, did climate change at the end of the last Ice Age wipe them out, or did both of these factors come into play? At any rate, we modern humans, in an amazingly short period of time, took the whole of Eurasia for ourselves and then settled North and South America as well, which up until then had not been inhabited. At the same time, there was a major evolutionary break in the animal world: the so-called megafauna, the big animals that roamed freely throughout Europe, Asia and the Americas, died off. Climate change is suspected to be the cause, but there are clear signs that hunting by modern humans also played a role.

So why am I talking about all this? What has this to do with the existential questions modern humans are asking themselves? In the article, the researchers said that modern humans possesses two characteristics which explain how we were able to so quickly spread out over all the continents. An essential trait was the ability to create tools and technologies for the hunt. Humans created the atlatl, a spear-thrower, which was a wooden socket into which the spear butt was placed, to make the throwing arm longer. With the spear- thrower, a spear could be thrown twice as far. This was the first tool made just for the hunting of big animals.

But the main assertion of the researchers dealt with modern humans' mental abilities. The development of certain social skills would apparently explain how we were able to spread out over the whole world with such astonishing speed. Around that time, we were already organized into groups clearly larger than the family unit.

People hunted in groups, and hunting in groups meant that we were more successful than the predators we were competing with. But there was also warlike aggression within these larger, organized groups. Within these early groups of modern humans, there was already a kind of solidarity that did not by and large exist in other species of early humans, an altruism among members of the group which increased the chances of individual survival.

There is evidence that groups had clearly defined borders defended through warfare. So stronger groups could conquer bigger territories, and less well-organized groups of other human species, or smaller and weaker groups of modern humans, had to give way. Modern humans, with their higher degree of cooperation, then spread out into still unoccupied territories and settled there. As soon as there was competition in a given territory, the weaker groups again had to retreat, and so modern humans swiftly spread out into new lands. The other species of humans were presumably under great pressure, nor were they as successful at settling new territories.

Our success as a species arises from two diametrically opposed abilities: the pronounced ability to live peacefully together within a group and the ability to act with coordinated aggression towards external threats, up to and including warfare.

This throws light on the human character, but there is darkness as well as light within. In spite of this, can we find the courage to look within ourselves, to see if these two extremes are still there? Can we see that we can be aggressive, but also our possibility of coming together? To help one another, and feel a bond with others who are not part of the tight family circle? Most of us feel the deep and abiding need to belong to a group. When we belong to a group, we have an identity, and we are prepared to protect our group from outside threats, even if we have to be aggressive. If we have an identity, the world is split in in two – there is me and there is the rest of the world, me and others.

As I was thinking about the article, it became clear to me that what we discover within ourselves, and cannot fully understand because there are so many contradictions, is part of our DNA: we owe our success as a species to our biology, to our genetic make-up. Animals are territorial by nature; they say: "This is my turf," and they defend it from others of their species. Birds say it in song: "I'm building my nest here, don't come too close. This is my hunting ground." The notion of territoriality existed among animals long before man showed up. But our ability to identify with a large group, a huge territory, and even a nation, appears to be uniquely human; and, as we know, somewhat dangerous.

All wars born of nationalism come from this "We"; from this nation that is more enlightened or more important than others, and that goes to war to increase in size at the expense of other nations. It is the identification with a group, with a nation, which unleashes this powerful energy that can be so destructive. Of course, this energy can be used to build as well as to destroy; but we only ever build for ourselves, never for others. This sense of belonging to a group is so much part of our make-up that it shapes our way of thinking and behaving.

Can we look at this more closely? Who are we, from the psychological point of view? Usually, when we ask ourselves this question, our life story comes up loud and clear. This is my story, the one I identify with: I come from such and such a place, this is where I was born, this is what I studied, these are my successes and failures, my life experiences, which I try to make sense out of as best I can. Our life stories are made up of memories and images, thought-pictures. What is of special significance when we speak of the ego is this: it never presents itself simply as a fact. There is always identification: I am that. These are my moral concepts, my rights, my needs, what sets me apart from others, my strengths and weaknesses, where I can't keep up, where others out-perform me, my shortcomings. Is this the stuff our ego is made up of – an endless string of identities?

And then the ego extends outwards to include my family, my partner, my children, my future, maybe my company, my property and then, finally - my nation. This means that while a bird, for example, limits itself to a little territory that it defends from others of its own species, in order to protect its food supply, we can extend our identities outwards, and there are no limits. Once we have established our identity and say, "This is mine, this belongs to me," we set about defending it. This is almost a reflex.

I can give you an example. Sometimes my name is misspelled. Almost every time this happens, I get slightly angry. "That's the wrong spelling! My name is not written like that!" Being quick to rise to anger shows that, to some degree, I still identify with my name.

Is it possible to directly observe these forms of identification, of which we have literally thousands? At least in the very moment when anger first shows itself? And is it possible to refrain from trying to explain it in words, and to work out why identifying is taking place? Seeing is enough, and the best place for it to happen is here, in the silence and stillness of retreat, when such moments arise in memory.

Can we also ask ourselves who was hurt, who was wounded, and who has to be defended? When we ask ourselves this question in all earnestness, most often no answer comes up, or we say to ourselves, "I was the one who was hurt, not somebody else. If I don't assert myself, what will become of me?"

But is it necessary to assert yourself? Of course, there are times when you must. Our very existence can be threatened by words, as when others threaten our place in society, or perhaps even threaten to exclude us from our social group. There was a time when being excluded from your group was almost a death sentence. Strong feelings of self-assertion are part of our nature, but the important thing is to see and understand what is happening, when this nearly automatic reflex leads us astray.

So is it possible to look directly at the words that hurt us, from one moment to the next? Who, or what, was hurt? Do we react in an appropriate manner?

I find myself remembering something that happened some years back. At the time, I had reached a point where I thought there were not many things left in my everyday life that could elicit feelings of being hurt. But then something happened, and this is perhaps as good a place as any to talk about it. In my free time, I do martial arts; the Korean style of karate, which is called Tae Kwon Do. One part of the discipline is called "form". It's like Tai Chi in that there is a series of carefully laid out movements you have to go through; but unlike Tai Chi, Tae Kwon Do requires a great deal of body strength. After years of training, I took part in a competition to see how I measured up.

This is what it looks like: you go out into a marked-off area in a gym, with a score-keeper at each corner of the performance area. Each judge has cards with numbers on them, which they hold up at the end of the performance, like in figure-skating. You get into position, go through the movements, and then the judges hold up their cards with their marks. At the end of my performance, I looked at the marks and thought: "Oh oh, not so good. I got marked low." It wasn't all that clear to me at the time, but I felt sort of sick to my stomach. And then I saw that another competitor, who I thought was nowhere near my level, had gotten better marks. My self-image took a beating. I thought that my performance was better and that I had been treated unfairly.

I think this is a pretty typical example of what we all go through at one time or another, but in my case, it took place in public. There were judges and spectators watching me, with a critical eye or wishing me well. You put yourself out there, do your best, and then feel under-appreciated. It doesn't matter whether the scores were fair or not. It seems to me that the feeling of being hurt doesn't really have much to do with the situation at hand.

So how do we handle this kind of hurt? Maybe you get stubborn and say: So be it. And then you train really hard with the hope of getting the recognition you deserve next time around. Often as not, we just chalk it up to experience and it becomes part of the long series of rejections and disappointments we have already experienced in life; and then we try to avoid such situations in the future. We concede defeat; and then most likely try to rationalize the whole thing, by way of explaining what really happened. We're not guilty, someone else is. The judges were incompetent, or they were using an unfair marking system. We're great rationalizers. In order to build ourselves up and be in the right, we interpret events in such a way as to put ourselves in the best possible light.

Or we do the opposite, and use the incident to bring ourselves down. We say: You were never very good anyway, and you're way too old to compete. Our mind is wonderfully, endlessly inventive at making sense of what happens to us. After a longish, mostly unconscious processing of what has happened, everything is made sense of and stored away in drawers as part of one's life story. And then, when we ask ourselves who we are, these many, carefully constructed stories come to the surface and we have the feeling: that's me.

But is this the truth? Do we weave our identities out of our life experiences, which we arrange in a certain sequence, to which we attribute value and worth, and which we indeed identify with? An illusion made up of images, a product of our imagination? Is everything caught up in an endless, repetitive loop with the accompanying emotions; and above all, with the need to assert oneself? To avoid future hurt, and with great intelligence, we build defensive walls around ourselves to shield us from situations that could cause us harm. We do not suffer bodily harm, but when the ego suffers, we react as though someone were trying to kill us.

Being attacked in this sense usually means that, in our everyday life, someone uses words that harm our self-image: the ego suffers. Now I am not that saying being attacked with words cannot cause us harm just because words are not actual knives. This is not what is meant. Slander or spiteful language can destroy a career and wreck relationships. You can't say that's harmless. But in spite of this, can we see how much we ourselves are part of what happens at such moments, and how simple a thing our identity is? What is being attacked is an idea, an image we have of ourselves. Is that all we are? Are we just a collection of ideas and images we identify with and defend? Is that what the ego is?

When we build up walls around ourselves to fend off attacks and stand up against others, our ability to show compassion or empathy is greatly hindered or outright stifled. Instead, we cultivate a feeling of separateness: this is what I am and these are my needs, and other people are quite separate from me. They can cause me harm and must be kept at a distance. I have to find ways to assert myself; I must defend myself from those around me.

The only attachments to others are within: these are my people; the people I care for; this is my group, my family, my sangha; these are the people I identify with. We shut out other people, those we call "others"; and the people who belong to our circle, who are part of this bloated entity we call the ego, these people we hold close.

So what are we, really? When we delve into the ideas and images we have of ourselves, and carefully examine the mental projections and all that which makes up our identity, we do not find a solid center, a still point. We identity with one thing today and another tomorrow. Personally, I have never found anything firm and solid among all the things I identify with, nor any stable underpinnings for my life.

But I have discovered that all this identifying and defending and the worry and aggressiveness that arises from it can come to a halt; and that all of my self-images can drop away, at least for a while. The feelings of separate-ness that shut out other people and make me feel alone, they too can dissolve into the silence.

We don't come to this awareness by perfecting the ego, by stopping up all the holes in our defenses and making it impossible for others to hurt us. It can happen, when our defenses fall and we accept that we can indeed be hurt by others. Suddenly, it becomes possible for us to function differently in our everyday lives. Without our trying to make it happen, our sense of separation from others disappears.

Effortlessly, warm feelings of affection and connectedness with others replace the impulse to defend and protect. When our vulnerability and the need to defend give way, our best qualities shine forth. We suddenly have empathy for others, and there is room for understanding our fellow humans.

Our bodies are like musical instruments that resonate effortlessly and in a perfectly natural way to the feelings of those around us. Nature has made us thus. There are mirror neurons in our brain. These are systems of cells that enable us to experience the emotions of others as if they were our own. I can see you're sad, and I can feel your sadness physically, in my very body: your sadness is present in me. This kind of emotional resonance manifests when there is no overlay of strong feelings of separation.

Without the possibility of understanding other people in this direct manner, through empathy and by literally experiencing the same feelings as those around us, true understanding between humans would just not be possible.

Words are very limited. This is especially clear when we communicate through the written word; emails and texting are fast and easy, and they often give rise to gross misunderstandings. This is just an exchange of thoughts. When we meet face to face, then there is a chance for direct understanding - there is body language we can pick up on. When there is openness and we allow ourselves to be vulnerable, then there is a coming together; and this finely tuned instrument, which is the body, feels what the person in front of us is experiencing. Then, genuine affection, empathy and love have a chance to manifest. They arise unbidden.

There are these wonderful Buddhist meditation practices in which the practitioner evokes feelings of loving-kindness towards others, indeed, towards the whole world. But this can only happen when there is inner stillness, when the whole structure of the ego is clearly seen and understood, and quiescent. When the walls come down, empathy and feelings of affection towards others are naturally present.

So, can we just be "no one"? Is it possible for our great network of identities and stories of self to become still, all by itself? You cannot make it happen, it has to take place all by itself. It happens when the structure of the ego is clearly seen, through and through, when not even the smallest particle remains.

All of a sudden, we don't take ourselves so seriously, and perhaps even smile at this great assemblage of identities and stories about ourselves. The body quiets down. There is a feeling of connectedness, and our feelings of loneliness and suffering go away. We live in relationship to others, without wanting anything from them. Indeed, without the need to get anything or be anything at all. Is there such a freedom, in which one doesn't have to be anything special? See for yourself if this is possible.

Maybe, after such a moment of stillness in which we find we are no one at all, there comes the fear that we may not be able to survive such openness and vulnerability. Are we really being delivered helplessly into the hands of some dark power? There is intelligence in this seeing, in this sensitive openness to hurt. We are not just blindly delivering ourselves in the hands of our enemies.

This doesn't mean that you just sit back and take it when someone tears into you. When there is something which has to be done, this can be seen; and then our actions come from the clarity of seeing and not from the ego, purely and simply. Our built-up ego leads us to create barriers between ourselves and others, and to create defensive strategies to keep others at a distance and protect us. This is what isolates us from others, what makes us unhappy and disconnected; and not the clarity of insight which comes from knowing what has to be done in the moment.

Sitting here in the hall, breathing quietly, seeing the sunlight, being aware of our bodily sensations and the people around us – who or what else more do we need? We don't have to be anyone special. It is enough to simply be a part of this amazing stream of life, to not feel apart from it, not wanting anything, nothing lacking.

Rosehips in the sunlight

(Photograph by Stephan Bielfeldt)

Day 4: What Sustains Us?

06 October 2016

Autumn had arrived, and it brought with it a cold and biting wind that cut right through me as I walked through the little park. The grass was wet and I felt a chill, even though I was wearing warm boots and an insulated jacket. This feeling of discomfort lingered a while, and all of a sudden I heard the geese far overhead. A moment later a big flock of geese came into view. There must have been a hundred of them. They were being carried along by strong winds and kept breaking into constantly changing V-shapes of about twenty birds each.

They were constantly talking to one another; the lead bird honking first and the others answering his call, as though they were saying, "We're still here, we're keeping up!" It really touched me. They were flying with a purpose, these birds making their way south, fleeing the cold and lack of food up here in the north. They were so strong and determined, and at the same time vulnerable and so sweet. I was very moved, and really felt I was one with these birds that were so full of life! At the same time, I felt a strong feeling of joy; and for a moment, I too was part of the flock flying south.

Someone in the group asked: "This longing we have for some kind of spiritual nourishment, a coming home, an opening up of the heart. . . Is this just a longing, or is there really someplace within where we can experience true fulfillment, that is one and whole and where there is no separation from others, a place where the desire to be other than we are is quiescent, where all our conflicts are resolved? Is there such a thing as a place that is sacred, holy even, because we become whole when we are there? Or is it just a place we long for; and when we find ourselves longing for this place, we feel apart, unfulfilled, incomplete; always trying to get there but never reaching our goal. Can we get there? If so, how?"

Instead of answering right off, let us take a look at the question. Where exactly do we find ourselves? What kind of world do we live in? Let's look at this together to see how we perceive the world, and how our understanding of the world constantly changes over time, but also for us personally as we get older. The world we live in today, and that we accept as true, has become endlessly bigger and ever more infinite. Science has given us many answers about who we are and where we are; but science has not united us in brotherly love, has it? Quite the contrary: finding ourselves adrift in infinite space gives us a feeling of being utterly insignificant.

Our sun finds itself on the edge of a galaxy, one of millions, an average star in a spiral galaxy made up of hundreds of billions of stars. It will burn for billions of years until it is completely consumed, and then go dark. Our little planet Earth circles the sun; and down here on Earth, our little circumscribed lives play out. This great expanse of space and time is immeasurably vast. We now know that the universe came into being about 13 ½ billion years ago in what we call The Big Bang. We live in the midst of an explosion, in an immense vastness of space that is expanding outwards ever faster, so fast that the light of The Big Bang has still not travelled all the way across. Even our biggest telescopes are unable to bring the most distant reaches of the universe into view; because, in theory, only the objects the light from which has already reached us may be seen.

When astronomers turn their mightiest telescopes, like the Hubble, onto areas of what appears to be empty space to the naked eye and even in smaller instruments, and collect the light long-enough, countless thousands of galaxies (like our Milky Way) swim into view, billions of light years away. We can see our sister galaxy with binoculars right here in our little park, if you stand out on the grass.

The Andromeda Galaxy is two and a half million light years away, just a fuzzy speck in the night sky, quite un-remarkable; but it is a galaxy containing hundreds of bil-lions of stars, even more than our galaxy contains. We look out from our Milky Way, made up of hundreds of billions of stars, at an even bigger Milky Way.

Endless space and time, because the light we get from the Andromeda galaxy left there two and half million years ago. It looks like all this has nothing at all to do with our little lives down here on Earth. How can we feel at one with such an immense universe? Can this possibly be a place where we feel at home?

Who is asking this question? Let us turn our regard in-wards and look at our physical being. We all live in a body, or are a body, as far as we can see. What we do know is that this body is a marvel. It is made up of countless cells, the endless and complex renewal of which is hard for us to grasp. There are hundreds of billions of cells just in the brain; that is a little galaxy all in itself.

Every year thousands upon thousands of scientific articles are published in journals that deal with neuro-science, but only a fraction of them will add to our understanding of how the brain actually works. Whether science will ever establish how our thoughts, feelings and actions come into being, is most questionable. It would appear that our understanding of these matters remains superficial. Especially eminent scientists are often modest in the face of all they do not know and understand.

Do the answers of science bring us a feeling of belonging or of Oneness? Many of us, on the contrary, experience fear in the presence of that which can neither be known nor understood. What science can communicate though, is astonishment and awe before the complexity and immensity of nature. And this also teaches us that it is presumptuous to say, "I am the master of this body," as though one could be in command of that which one neither can control nor, even in the most rudimentary way, understand.

But how can we find something to hold onto? Where can we find Oneness, where can we abide and be loved? Can religious belief give us the answers?

Whatever our religious beliefs may be, there is much division of opinion. For some, belief is made up of rules for living and sacred words and sacred texts, which are accepted as absolute truth. For others, it consists of reaching an understanding of our own existence which cannot be explained in a logical manner. Etymologically, "religio" means "respect", but also "mindful". It points to finding a link to the Divine, a link we may have had at one time and then lost. Is such a thing possible? Can we find a path to the Divine through belief? If logic can't help, then what can?

Sometimes I think of Taoism, in which the concept of "Tao" describes the mystery that is the ground of all existence. Anything that can be said about the Tao is not the absolute Tao [2]. The true Tao lies beyond being and not-being. It is ungraspable, mysterious, and is neither being nor not-being. It belongs neither to things that exist nor to things that do not exist. Our thinking mind throws up its hands and can go no further. So what does all of this mean? Our thinking mind stumbles and comes to a halt. It can go no further. And this is perhaps the most important lesson to come out of these mysterious philosophies: namely that thought, and all ideas of self and of understanding of the self, have their limits, and there comes a time when they can go no further. They come to a stop as it becomes clear that they simply don't work. The thinking mind works just fine in our everyday life; but when it comes to delving into the sacred and exploring the nature of the universe, it is condemned to failure.

And so we come back to our original question: what sustains us? Is there such a thing as a place that is whole and sacred; a place of Oneness, beyond thought and all imagining?

With this we come to the notion of enlightenment, which occupies a central role in Buddhism. And what is enlightenment? Does enlightenment mean that we have reached our goal? Are the fires of our longing extinguished? When we imagine what enlightenment is like, we summon up beautiful pictures of it. The burden of care is lifted off our shoulders and we earn fundamental understanding. We are in control, and endless joy and endless energy wells up

---

[2] Laotse. Herausgegeben von Lin Yutang. Frankfurt am Main, Hamburg, 1955, S. 37.

from within. That's the way it is described in many books on Buddhism. And so our sense of longing has found something new to long for: Enlightenment, something that in one fell swoop explains how this amazing world works.

Can we see that these imaginings are just mental constructs? Everything I have said thus far comes from the thinking mind. I have used many words to describe, to give examples and to create images. But what is the real thing? What is it that is not words and description? If it exists, is it something we can possess? Usually we want to attain something, is it not so? We live in expectation: we expect to get something from a wise being, or through strenuous effort, or by the grace of God. Working hard at my meditation comes from the idea that I can attain something through strenuous effort.

Every image we create gives us a burst of energy and makes us feel good, for a while. This is how ideas and concepts work. After a while, the idea or the concept has lost its appeal and not given us anything; so we start looking for something new.

We are always on the lookout for something that will satisfy our sense of longing. When we find that we have no real kinship or link with other people who are engaged in spiritual work, then we turn to family and friends, or to husband and wife. We assume that, when they cannot provide us with this feeling of Oneness, then neither can anyone else.

Relationships based on conditions and requirements on both sides often lead to conflict. Having different opinions and expectations, and defending different positions, often makes us feel separated from each other. When there is disagreement, we become suspicious of others and take it for granted that they have their own agendas; so we go back to our own personal, selfish pursuits. You go your way and I go mine. It's important to look out for yourself because no one else will. Sometimes you have to toot your own horn; no one will do it for you!

It's important to look out for yourself because warm feelings of love and of Oneness always arise from within. They come from the heart. Also, we treat others the same way we treat ourselves. When we don't like ourselves, when we are hard on ourselves and put ourselves down and have low self-esteem, then we carry these feelings over to others. How can we have a feeling of harmony and Oneness with others? We have a driving need, an urge, to belong. We want to have relationships in which we feel loved and understood and in which we can abide. But this only comes about when a feeling of connectedness and the ability to love are already present.

And we still don't have an answer to our question: is there something that is truly holy, our true home? Is there really and truly a sacred place or way of being, within which we are indeed holy and complete; and there is nothing lacking?

Everything I have said thus far has pointed to limits and limitations. Perhaps my words have made it clear that all of our efforts to find Oneness, through others or through science, philosophy or religion, get us nowhere other than to point to where we must look.

Can we find it within? The question then becomes: Who are we? What is the self? Yesterday we were saying that the self is a collection of ideas, images and identities. This cannot be the source of the sacred, this construct of the self with which we identify and which is separate from everything else. This is the very opposite of Oneness and the source of all disunity. But what is the true self? Is there something behind the self-construct?

If we truly want to find out, we must be still and listen to the confusion within. This is what we are doing here in retreat: listening, becoming aware. Is it possible not to hold onto whatever manifests; but just look and see what comes up, from one moment to the next? Can we just see if we can quiet down and become still? Can this inner world of mental noise, of thought and images, always front and center, always obscuring the awareness of this moment – can we somehow change course and veer away from it, so that we find ourselves grounded in silence and stillness? A state of stillness in which thoughts appear and disappear, like ripples on the surface of a pool, in which images and feelings are like cat's paws on the water. Impulses do not become actions; rather they are seen and then dissipate: we remain quiet and still and there is simply awareness, no need for an identity. We behold what is, from one moment to the next.

Everything takes place in this stillness. We are beholding that which is there. But who is it that is looking? Is there someone looking? When there is stillness, then the observer also is just a ripple on the surface of the water; it comes and goes. What I used to identify with is now seen to be just a sequence of thoughts and feelings that change from one moment to the next; they come and go. When stillness is there, then everything becomes imbued with this quiet, living energy.

Concepts and imaginings can cause so much fear and worry, the fear that we may soon die or become an invalid or that something or another will happen to us. Can we see that these fears are made up of thoughts and feelings that come and go in the Great Silence, that they are not our identity and that they are not going to gobble us up?

Is such a thing possible? We do not know what death is. We only know what life is, from the very moment of birth on. We know what death is only because we see it happening to others, never having experienced it ourselves.

So many ideas, concepts, and images. We see ourselves as a doddering old person in a wheelchair in an old-age home, ringing the bell and no one comes. Such images come and go. There are all these fears and worries we have about the future and about what will become of us. Is it possible for us not to be overwhelmed by all of this? By which I mean, is it possible for our awareness not to be completely filled up with all these fears and imaginings?

Can they occur and leave the waters undisturbed? There is then a state of Stillness-in-Being and the possibility to see the endless parade of thought and image for what it is: just an endless show, an ever-changing display of memories, accompanied by feelings.

Can we become more still here in retreat? When it is clear that all this worrying about oneself, about not being loved or accepted, can be seen for what it really is: just a stream of images and feelings here in the body? When we are in silence, then our awareness can flourish. We recognize the feeling or image for what it is, and it subsides and fades away.

So who are we? Do we have to BE something? As long as we are trying to reach a goal, as long as there is this longing to find the sacred and the holy, then there is separation. When there is true stillness and we recognize our longing for what it is, as a feeling or an emotion, then there is clarity, there is awareness, and we are present.

The German mystic Johannes Tauler speaks of how to go about this work a number of times in his writings, and I should like to put what he says into my own words: "If you want to know God, then you must make room for Him." This is a radical notion, an inner revolution. He means that all these ideas and feelings and images and emotions that make up the self, have to be quiescent so that there is space, room for the sacred to enter in [3].

Does all of this make any sense to you? What is there when we are not anything at all, when this underlying Stillness is there and everything that occurs is just a flowing energy, like waves on the surface of the water that come and go, and the waters are not disturbed? When the Stillness deepens, identity is absent; there is no self, no one there at all. And with this, no one seeking anything at all.

I just thought of something the Buddha is supposed to have said. To paraphrase, he said that he had achieved nothing from complete and full enlightenment, and that indeed this is what constitutes full enlightenment [4]. Is it possible not to be anything or to try to get anything? Is it possible to be no one, and just be with this amazing energy

---

[3] Johannes Tauler. Predigten. Band I. Uebertragen von Georg Hofmann. 3. Auflage. Einsiedeln 1987, S. 19.
[4] Huang Po: The Zen Teaching. On the Transmission of Mind. Translated by John Blofeld. New York 1994, S35.

grounded in stillness and silence? One moment we want something or don't want something, and then the wanting just goes away. But when no one is there, there are no needs or desires, nothing is lacking; so there is no sense of longing. Is this the place where we feel one and complete, where there is just this amazing flow of energy in stillness, a flowing of moments from one to the next and time does not exist?

Can we also not look at what we want or at what we get, but rather do just the opposite; and try to see what there is that we don't need, or how much we can do without? Can we become less and less, here in meditation?

When this quiet, deep energy and stillness in which everything takes place is there in the foreground, then cares and worries and needs suddenly disappear. We cannot say what enlightenment is or is not, or whether we have experienced a Unio Mystica – a Mystical Union – or not, because we are no longer there. This Stillness is beyond all concepts and descriptions. A description of it would be a desire to possess it, to hold onto it, which brings us right back to thinking and rationalizing.

We are speaking of a place that cannot be reached through someone, through a person, like me. We enter into this inconceivable all-encompassing Awareness and Stillness where nothing is lacking. We are lost in it. Are we afraid of getting lost? We are inclined to hold fast onto our sense of self, which is a cage; but there is no need to be frightened, for there is no danger when it becomes truly still, even if it feels like dying.

So what is it like right now? Is there still a fear of losing oneself? Can the fear be seen as a cat's paw on the still surface of a pool, as something transitory that comes into being and then dissipates when we abide in Stillness?

Look for yourself! Can you feel the relief? In the simple Present there is nothing to attain, nothing is missing. Awareness is enough.

Cranes flying over Schlagsuelsdorf
(Photograph by Rainer Simmelbauer)

Day 5: Conflict and Decision Making

07 October 2016

An astonishing intensity of feeling of Oneness can reveal itself in one's daily life. Just a little while ago, before I started on my way over to the meditation hall to give the talk, I was walking in the rain with my big umbrella. Looking back, it's a very clear memory: with every step I made a splash; and in spite of my umbrella and my waterproof jacket, the feeling of wet skin. The wet was coming through the arms of my jacket and my shoes were soaked - but there was no one there complaining. The rain was drumming on the umbrella, birds were chirping from the shelter of the bushes: they hadn't been expecting anyone on the path! My eyes took in the pond. It was like it was divided into two parts. One side was rippled by the breeze, and on the other side the water was smooth and still. The line separating the two moved with every gust of wind. On the still side, bushes and weeds were reflected back like in a mirror, and the raindrops were making circles on the still surface of the water. There was a deep stillness, even now it appears as I remember the scene.

The endless stream of thought that accompanies our every waking moment and every event became a trickle. The orchestration of thought was just not there. There was no thinking: "Dang! Rain all day! You can't even go for a walk without getting wet!" Direct seeing was there instead, and this replaced knowing and thinking. What was seen and experienced was without commentary. Single thoughts came up but could not break the flow. One thought did flicker into awareness: "What am I going to say in the talk?", but it hardly aroused any feeling of concern or anxiety. The stillness remained undisturbed. I resumed walking. Was this a conscious decision? Who is in charge of this body-mind? It is so astonishing that everything takes place without me having to steer and lead the way.

In thinking and talking, it is always so; as though it were perfectly clear who "I" is and that I am the one acting. Here in group dialogues, people do not always agree when the "I" comes up for discussion. People's opinions differ, and their personal experiences also.

The "I" is first and foremost a concept. We can each of us find out for ourselves if there is an "I" beyond thought and concept, and we have the time to look at this in retreat.

Let's put the question into words, here and now, this very morning: Can we go through life without an "I" concept? Or to put it more clearly, without an active "I" concept? Can we go through our daily lives without constant self-reference, or is this impossible? Of course, it's easy to go for a walk in silence and say to yourself: "I don't need an 'I' to do so." What is it like, in our everyday life, at work for example, when everyone around us is making demands of us and we have to produce? How do we cope when we're not "I" oriented and when we do not, from one moment to the next, distinguish between self and other; when others expect things of us? How can I get my due and meet my own needs? How can we defend ourselves, when there is no difference between you and me?

When we perceive everything as being One, as an unbroken stream of life, how do we go about getting through our everyday life? Here in retreat, we can indeed experience how life is an unbroken, flowing stream, even if it is only for a moment: unexpectedly the living stream of life appears, and there is no longer a separate self. We become part of this unbroken stream of being, like a drop of water returning to the ocean. Is this something that we can only experience here, in the shelter of retreat? Are we completely lost in the demands of everyday life when we lose our sense of self?

It's important to understand that every effort to defend the self, every self-directed action, here in retreat and in our everyday lives, begins with an innocent perception. The self-centered reaction to it may come afterwards. It makes a difference to perceive that there is a real need - or realize we're just talking to ourselves. If we don't want to be controlled by our old convictions and programming, we have to see if the same old thought patterns are still at work, maybe a little voice saying: "You have to eat everything on your plate. I've always believed this." Such a saying doesn't stop us from piling food up on our plate though, does it? When we simply stay with the perception and this is a state of awareness, we feel how hungry we really are before we serve ourselves and we don't take more than we need. Is it possible to see how hungry we really are without thinking about how big an appetite we have? Can we serve ourselves without making a thing out of it? My plate, my appetite, how big my appetite is and whether half a plateful is enough. Can we act without being carried along by thoughts of self and "me" in our everyday lives?

Is it possible for us to see what we really need, and distinguish true needs from images and concepts rooted in the self and ego? This is what is called a clear mind.

But who is making this distinction, if it isn't the "I"? Do we need an "I" to decide for us when we do something? If

I'm not the one making the decisions and distinctions, then who is doing it? It's easy to get confused and to go astray when we address this question with the intellect alone. Rather let us just look, from one moment to the next, how our decisions and actions come about.

We like to say: "Having given the matter a great deal of thought, I made my decision." How do we make a decision after thinking about something? Let's take a look at how the whole process works, through the lens of memory. In such cases we have the time to reflect and this is important because it can be a life-changing decision. Perhaps you're thinking of starting a family, or maybe of doing just the opposite, of breaking up with your partner and ending a relationship. Maybe you're thinking of changing professions and going to work for another company.

What takes place within when such decisions are made? How do we go about making up our minds? We've all been through it. We've all gone through rough patches, when we are under great pressure and have to make up our minds; and once we decide, there's no going back.

It's interesting to see how such decision-making is first preceded by a great outpouring of thought: we imagine how our new life will be in a great flurry of thought and image.

"What will it be like once I've decided? How will things be different? What are the plusses and minuses? What do I get out of it?" We try to picture what it will be like, and a whole landscape of images and stories and memories of past experiences come up, with their attendant feelings and emotions. We don't think of just the good things – we picture every possible problem and difficulty. "If I give up my full-time job, what will happen to the house? Will I have to sell it?" We see ourselves miserable and unhappy in a run-down rented room in some dive, and a host of images and thoughts come up and get added to the ones that already cause us such distress. A lot of the time we go through every heaven and hell imaginable even before we take the first step in deciding what to do. The only thing left out of the process is what actually takes place later on.

In all of this thinking and imagining and to-ing and fro-ing, there's not much clarity. Too many known and un-known factors have to be taken into account to come to appropriate solutions by use of logic alone. Most of the time we don't know enough and so cannot come to a log-ical decision. We're often confused and don't know how we should proceed; but we act nonetheless, and this oc-curs when there is an impulse, an urge, that pushes us for-ward.

We don't know where this impulse comes from; but we can try to see, can't we? Suddenly the impulse arises and we act; but at the last minute, fears and uncertainties come up and get bigger and bigger and they get in the way. They upset the applecart. There's pushback, and what we've be-gun to do just goes off the rails. When we look back, we can't for the life of us figure out what happened.

Now we don't always find ourselves in such an extreme and chaotic quandary over coming to a decision, but maybe you can remember finding yourself in such a posi-tion once or twice in your life. It's worth noting that, in looking back, we often explain or rationalize a decision we have made in order to better understand what we have done and find other ways of explaining our actions. Even when we suspect that we didn't behave all that rationally we pretend that we arrived at our decision after a long process of deliberation: "That was my decision and I had reasons to do what I did." That's what we say. We can always find reasons for our decisions, but where do they really come from? They come from images and stories we make up all the time, and from the feelings that accompany them. Ultimately, our actions arise from feelings and impulses; and we don't always know what comes along with those impulses and feelings. Instead of there being a free and independent "I" acting on its own and making decisions for rational reasons, a complex mix of transitory influences and moments of resolve (of which we may be aware or unaware) come into play and set this body-mind into motion. Is this just my own personal theory or observation?

Look for yourself! Where is the "I" in your decision-making process? Can we perceive an entity making the decision, or is all of this just the play of mental constructs?

The confusion and lack of clarity in our decision making actually stems from the fact that we ourselves don't observe how it all takes place. Is it possible to bring understanding and feelings into some kind of harmony? On the one hand, we have the thinking mind that understands; and when we have enough time and a given problem has a practical side to it, trying to understand it in a systematic and thoughtful manner can throw a lot of light on the matter. Maybe you want to buy a house and you are looking at several properties and must choose one. Then it's only logical to make a list of all the advantages and disadvantages of the different houses. You have to make a detailed list of the costs involved in order to make an informed decision, but that is not the end of the decision-making… Because on the other hand, when the practical factors have been looked at, feelings come into play: we can simply observe which feelings are involved in the making of our decision.

When we look inwards in a meditative manner, and bring into awareness all the thoughts and images and feelings that reveal themselves in the light of our understanding in this manner, often the decision is made all on its own. It becomes clear to us what we know and what we cannot know, what we like and what our fears are, without any-one being there who is doing something or making some-thing happen. And there arises within a harmonious com-ing together of seeing, understanding and action. Making up our mind seems easy and there is no conflict. Of course, we have no way of knowing if afterwards we'll say that we've made the right decision.

Now I'd like to talk about another kind of decision – deci-sions that give you no time to think things through: you have to decide in a fraction of a second. Even though you must act quickly, there can still be observation. It seems like there was no decision involved; there was just an ac-tion taken. Awareness seems to come in only when the ac-tion or movement has already taken place. For example, you're setting the table and a glass slips out of your hand and you catch it before it can fall to the floor. You drop the glass and you grab it in one smooth movement, and only then do you see that you caught the glass in mid-air. Is that not amazing? Who did it? If we carefully observe what took place, we see that no one made a decision; there was no decision involved, nor do we remember having made a decision. We have the glass in our hand and we don't know how it happened. Our reaction, the lightning-fast, highly complex act that took place in a flash came from what we call the body-mind.

It would be absurd to say that I made a conscious decision to grab the glass. What we can observe in such situations is that an action has taken place and was completed, but no one performed the action. Many of our actions take place in this manner, and in these cases we really cannot say: "I did this. I decided to act." Is this a source of confusion, or can such a realization throw light on our lives and actions?

When we carefully observe what we do, it becomes clear that the whole world, with its complex interactions, has an effect on our body-mind and actions take place; which means that we are not the ones making decisions and doing things. Everything is tied in with everything else, everything has an effect on everything else; and out of all this, things take place – what happens, happens.

Usually we believe that we personally make decisions and then act upon them. I find it a great relief to realize that actions do not originate with the ever-present "I" but take in the broader context of our whole being. How often we find ourselves displeased and in distress over things we have done, and experience feelings of guilt because we got it all wrong. "How could something like that happen to me? How could I have been so dumb?" We identify with our decisions and assume all the guilt if things go wrong. "It's my mistake, I screwed up, I'm the one at fault." Granted, the action arose in this body-mind; but so much more comes into play! No one carries the weight of the guilt by himself, and even this is just another representation of what is happening.

People often ask me if we have to forgive everything and even put up with murder and extreme violence, because there is no one can be found guilty. They say they don't want to live in such an awful world, and that an "I" is needed just to cope with guilt.

From the theoretical point of view, it gets confusing; so let's stick with direct observation. When we've done something, it's perfectly possible to look back and see what we have done. This is what we perceive: "Yes, this act arose from this body-mind, though many other people and circumstances added to it. But ultimately, this body-mind was the place where it came into action." With this insight, it only seems right for us to accept responsibility for our action. This is what it means to be responsible.

Can we answer for what we do without wanting to misconstrue what we have done and throw the blame onto someone else? Isn't it clear that we are directly involved, in our own eyes and before others? This is what is meant when we say that we accept responsibility. Accepting responsibility is appropriate and enough in itself. It isn't a matter of sin and guilt and self-condemnation. Our courts proceed from the assumption that humans have a free will and choose between good and evil; but when we look closely, we see that this is a vulgar simplification of real life. To accept responsibility for our actions seems to me to be only right. It is a necessary and unavoidable part of the social contract and unavoidable if we are to live together in society.

Now guilt and responsibility are not the same thing. We often act out of ignorance or are influenced by strong feelings; so sometimes we can't see straight, or we're overwhelmed by circumstances. Such behavior is only human and not bad or a reason to feel guilty. I am speaking here of the harm we may have caused others. We can see what we have done and try to make up for it. Bad intentions can arise when we're led astray by jealousy, envy or greed. It isn't easy; but what is best for us all is to be aware of the forces at play in everyone, in you and me, in one's self and in others. The same forces are at play within us all. This is the true meaning of awareness. Images of guilt and sin and fear of punishment often prevent us from seeing things clearly.

For me, it is a matter of awareness, an opening up of the self to the truth. We can become aware of all sources, of all information, without attributing value or identifying with it all. Is it possible to see what is happening and how we behave, me and you? Can we come to this direct insight, see what is happening from moment to moment and see the forces at work behind our behavior? When this is possible, then we come to have a better understanding of others. When we see with open eyes and our astonishing mirror neurons allow us to feel what others are feeling directly, then we are receiving information first hand. Then we can see more deeply into what is taking place. When the "I" we are so fixated on is inactive for even a moment, then all of our other concepts and feelings of guilt and judgement are in abeyance and this body-mind becomes a finely tuned instrument capable of grasping and understanding reality with amazing precision and sensitivity. Is such a thing possible? Can this take place today or on any day? See for yourself!

There is another question I would like to look at, one that often comes up when we have seen that this "I" can be quiet and still, and that we are nonetheless capable of making decisions and acting in a normal fashion. Is there such a thing as free will? The question has been much discussed by natural scientists and psychologists in recent years, and there is much disagreement. Brain specialists mostly agree that the brain unconsciously takes in all the available information from the outside world and from the memory and informs us; which is to say it informs the conscious person we are, of the decision being made and at the same time confirms the existence of the "I" who is making the decision. The time lag we do not pick up on; the brain compensates by correcting it. Many philosophers, on the other hand, state that humans are free and make their decisions freely and logically, and for good reasons. This, they say, is self-evident.

What can we observe within ourselves, here and now, without seeking guidance from philosophers or brain specialists? Fortunately, amazing things are right at hand. For example, we have a body-image; and when we move or raise a finger, there is a feeling of intent. We notice this when we compare such a moment with unintentional movements like a reflex, for example. Doctors used to use a little rubber hammer to test our reflexes. A littler tap on the tendon, just below the kneecap and the leg bounces up all by itself. We don't consciously decide to kick upwards – the movement is automatic.

One thing is clear: in the image we have of our bodies and our movements, we make a distinction between intentional and unintentional movements. We recognize the difference by saying to ourselves: "I'm doing such and such", or "This action is taking place all on its own; I'm not doing it". Of course, it is not given to us to observe whether unknown mental processes have taken place before we become aware of what has happened.

But we can observe more complex actions. Every thought and image has an effect upon the body: something is released - emotions, feelings, movements and actions arise and they all influence one another. Thoughts are accompanied by their own suite of feelings that influence the thoughts that come after, and they lead to further actions, and this leads to a new series of thoughts and feelings and moments of awareness. All this can be observed, but the only thing missing is the doer behind these complex happenings. Instead of a doer, there is the ego, being a thought of self (the "I") which is connected to the doer; but this is not the answer to the question of who is in charge. And who is in charge of this complex inner world? Who is in the driver's seat? It's hard to throw light on this question, but maybe the question isn't all that important after all.

All the conflict that gives rise to the abiding fear we have of not being free, of being like robots with no inner worth, as far as I can see comes from theoretical concepts and does not match up with what we observe directly in ourselves from moment to moment. We are not robots, but complex living organisms. So, what is real freedom? Does it not come from a feeling that we are free? We feel free when we don't feel constrained or that someone is ordering us about and telling us what we can do and not do and makes up our mind for us. When we are free to express ourselves, when someone isn't always telling us what we may do and not do – this is freedom. There are clear examples of things that make us feel free; and the feeling that we can raise our hands, freely and intentionally, is a moment of awareness in so far as our complex physiology allows us to understand what is happening.

Our amazing body-mind is so constituted that we can live and act and do astounding things, like play the piano. I can't play the piano, but I've heard that experienced pianists can see themselves seated at the keyboard playing. Hitting the right key at the right moment – is this a conscious decision? It's absurd to think that every contact between finger and keyboard is a separate conscious decision! Long hours of practice make it possible for the fingers to fly over the keyboard all on their own, and the pianist has the freedom to shape the music and to interpret a piece with great feeling. How far removed is the art of the pianist from the chimes of a mechanical clock! Our wondrous body-mind acts all on its own, with amazing skill and ability, spontaneously and in the moment, and it is an endless wonder how living music comes into being!

When we look inward, we see there is no separate entity in our head that is the source of our actions, that controls and directs. As far as we can perceive, our actions arise from everything that comes together in the moment.

Is there such a thing as a correct action? We've already spoken about responsibility and guilt. When is a decision the correct decision? Are we always running the risk of making the wrong move because there is no one who knows what's best? We've already said that a thousand elements come into play and many unknown factors as well, and that they all have their say in what we do. "Am I doing the right thing?" is a question that comes up as we act and when we are in the midst of doing something and after we have acted also. There is uncertainty. Looking back, doubts arise. "That was the wrong decision. I didn't think the thing through. I acted from my convictions or because of my feelings. Now I can see that it was the wrong thing to do!" Is that inevitable?

Is there such a thing as acting with a clear mind and without uncertainty? It seems to me that it is possible to act with clarity when you see things clearly; and there is clarity when we are truly aware and present, and not overwhelmed by our feelings, and thoughts do not go round and round in a closed loop automatically. When there is awareness and you see things clearly, then there is true intelligence at work – the intelligence that knows and understands the meaning of that which is perceived. Feeling and thought are in harmony. And contradictions are resolved. We can then really see this clarity at work.

When we are aware and fully in the moment, in the here and now, we can have a direct experience of this clarity at work. We ask a question and then silently listen. We might ask:" What should I do in this situation?", and then look at things with this inner clarity.

Thoughts and feelings rise up out of the stillness: we are present and can see what is happening but we don't do anything. We are merely present, and not caught up in old storylines, not overwhelmed by old feelings or trapped in a closed loop of thought and memory. In a moment of clarity, there is no conflict between thought and feeling; and the action that comes out of this insight is clear and free of hesitation.

Our usual to-ing-and-fro-ing is not there because there is listening, and the body flows along with the action being taken. Seeing and making a decision, and then acting upon it, all flow together: they are practically one and the same; and there is a fine energy and the joyous knowledge that the right decision has been made and the right action taken. Maybe in looking back, the thought will arise that you made a mistake, but in the moment, when you were acting, it was the right decision and there was no conflict. Maybe in looking back you will say: "It was the right thing to do at that time," and there are no regrets.

Is it possible for us, in the course of this week of silent retreat, to examine how we arrive at a decision? Is making the right decision and doing the right thing, out of awareness, just a theory of mine; or can we all do this? Can there really be a harmonious way of feeling, thinking and acting? Can things be clear to us in the next moment, without the intrusion of an "I"?

When we start thinking about right and wrong, arguments and thoughts rise to the surface one after the other; we are easily led astray and there is no awareness amidst this welter of feelings. We have more space when we look at things in the here and now. Memories are seen as memories together with what is actually taking place right in front of us. We see things differently when we are in the here and now. Instead of purely intellectual processes coming into play, we are also able to observe the constantly changing parade of feelings and emotions passing through us. Sometimes there are circumstances we cannot grasp intellectually, but we are able to understand them through our feelings. We always seek to understand what is taking place with the thinking mind, but right action cannot occur if we ignore our feelings.

And why do we always have to do the right thing? When we look deeper, we are really asking if there is such a thing as a right way to live; and so we come to the very root of all our wondering and questioning: what is the meaning of life? Is there even such a thing?

As long as there is a thinking self at work, we have our goals, we want to accomplish something in life and we cling to our opinions. But if we see the "I", the thinking self, as a bundle of thoughts and definitions and identities from within, can we still say this life has a meaning? I can neither affirm nor deny, but an example comes to mind. Let's look at this from the point of view of a tree rather than from the point of view of a human being. The buds appear early in the season; actually, you can see them already appearing in winter. In May the buds open and tender green leaves appear and caterpillars are feeding on them. In the fall, around now, the leaves turn gold and yellow; and they die off and fall to the ground. They go through an amazing life-cycle, as the dead leaves become soil and maybe in a year or two, the tree draws nourishment from this very soil and makes new leaves.

What is the meaning of the life of a leaf? Maybe we find the question meaningless, but let us just take a closer look.

"What is the meaning of a leaf?" – that is how we think and question things. Why do we have leaves anyway? When the sunlight falls on the leaf, photosynthesis takes place and the tree receives sustenance and can grow. A leaf is not an individual but very much part of a whole, namely a tree. The tree creates the leaves and then discards them when winter sets in and brings with it the cold and dark. We can go further and ask: "What is the meaning of a tree?"

The tree grows from a small seed, grows over many years or even centuries, becomes old and knotty and then dies and falls over. Fungi sprout from the rotting wood and plants grow out of the humus. We say also that a tree is part of nature and not an individual and separate entity.

So perhaps a tree has no individual meaning or purpose other than being part of a forest and part of the cycle of life.

Are we really all that different from leaves and trees? We are born; we don't know where we come from; we grow up; we move around and live in different places; and in an inconceivably short space of time from the point of view of our planet or of the cosmos, we die; our cells disintegrate; and we become sustenance for other life forms.

Where are the great things we have to accomplish? Where is our meaning? Maybe we have written books and changed history. But how important is humankind on this insignificant little planet at the edge of this gigantic galaxy we call the Milky Way, which is just one galaxy in billions? The question of meaning just does not have any significance when we talk about human life and existence. But it works when we talk about those things that are useful in our lives. Little things do indeed have meaning for us. What is the meaning of tools? With a hammer and nail, I can hang a picture. And what is the meaning of a car? I can drive to places with my car. But we speak about the meaning and purpose of things that do not serve any purpose. Looking for meaning only has meaning when we set limits: meaning and usefulness go hand in hand. Why should our lives have meaning? Why should life itself have meaning? Why should the cosmos have meaning beyond the wonder of existence? Is existence not itself a great wonder? Is it not a mighty wonder in itself that anything at all should exist?

For a long time, I have been asking myself if I have a purpose in this world, if there is something I must accomplish; and as I asked and looked at this question recently, I saw that I was harboring a certain assumption about myself that I had not looked at for a long time. I took it for granted that life must have a meaning. At that time, being a teacher was not part of the picture; but a retreat came and I found myself wondering what there is when one does not have a purpose in life. I asked myself: is it not enough to be what I am, right now?

Just be; and be aware that life itself is wondrous, here and now, without being separated from anything? Is it not enough to be borne along by the swinging arm of the galaxy through the cosmos that is beyond all understanding? Is it not enough to be part of this wondrous mystery? In that moment this was enough; and instead of the desire to be something, there was just the simple presence I would describe as clear and astonishing.

In truth, we are no one, in completeness and emptiness.

The pond in Schlagsuelsdorf Park
(Photograph by Stephan Bielfeldt)

Day 6: Awareness in Everyday Life

08 October 2016

After almost seven days of silence, we are approaching the end of our retreat. Soon we'll be returning to our everyday lives. Shall we, all together, look at the following question today: what difference is there really between our lives in retreat and our everyday lives back home?

Maybe you feel that there is a very big difference. A retreat is like an intense kind of holiday – time out, a downtime. The meaning is already in the word "retreat", which means pulling back and giving things up; and this is indeed an important part of what a retreat is, compared to a regular holiday in which we often try to do too much and to experience all we can cram into a brief holiday.

Outside experiences take up all our time. Can we ask ourselves what is so very different in a week given over to seeking out the stillness and the silence? For one thing, we're spending a whole week in a kind of protected place, a safe zone, where our every need is seen to. We don't have to worry about meals and we have a nice place to sleep. All of our daily needs are carefully taken care of, so that we have hardly anything that needs doing. There is plenty of space and free time - space in the true meaning of the word: room to move around in. You can go for a walk whenever you feel like it. Time is freed up, so you can do as you please, as the spirit moves you. There is no pressure from the outside, unless we create such pressures ourselves. All retreat activities are optional. There is nothing standing in the way of the peace and quiet, at least not from outside. You have the freedom of not having to do or be anything, which is in stark contrast to our everyday lives.

The most important thing is the silence. If you don't want to come to the talk, you can spend the whole week in complete silence. And should you choose to go to private meetings or the group dialogue, you still spend the greater part of the day in silence. This means that we have plenty of time to listen. As we go about our daily routine in retreat, we still communicate with one another, but without using words. We have the space to carefully observe and listen to this wordless communication. In the stillness and the silence, we can become more aware of what we spontaneously think about other people when, for example, we come together at meal times. We feel the connection we have with others, and sometimes a strong feeling of togetherness. We enter into a relationship with others without saying a word, and the feeling of togetherness can often lead to a feeling of Oneness.

To be able to be yourself, and be free of all outside obligations, and still be together with others – this is a special experience. And when we go back to our everyday lives – tomorrow already! – we are immediately struck by the difference. All we have to do is look carefully, and we see right away how much energy we spend on talking. There is a lot of pent-up energy in us after a week of silent retreat, and this energy is looking for an outlet. Some people just let it all out, but not everyone. It's perfectly alright to hold back and at least stay quiet on the way home.

As soon as we go back to our everyday lives, we at once realize how much less is demanded of us in a silent retreat. All the complex interaction with others, all the activities we are constrained to engage in: discussions, role playing, planning our daily activities - all of this falls away, or only takes place in the head, when you are in retreat. It is perfectly clear that we just have too much of everything in our everyday lives.

There are those who assert that our consciousness is without end; but this is a mistake, which is something we can easily see for ourselves. What we can perceive, recognize, and act upon in the moment is in no way limitless.

And how do we cope with this limiting of our consciousness? When we're overwhelmed and cannot consciously cope with what is there, our brain switches to automatic. We act, but without experiencing our thoughts and feelings and actions from one moment to the next, in the here and now. Without our "autopilot" we wouldn't be able to go about our daily business. Our incredible bodies have found amazing ways to get things done, efficiently and automatically. Various postures and physical activities like driving a car, are complex undertakings that are accomplished smoothly and easily, without our being fully aware; and this is a good thing.

I remember when I was learning how to drive how I had to consciously pay attention to signs and traffic lights; which means that I had to think of what I was doing before putting my foot on the brake pedal. I felt lost in heavy traffic and was only too glad to have the driving instructor next to me – more than once he prevented an accident from happening. We take it for granted that as we drive and keep our eyes on the traffic, we can let our minds wander and think about something else or listen to the radio or take a telephone call. We are so used to doing this that we don't even notice. Is it possible for us to stop for a moment and consciously observe what is happening when we're on automatic? You can do it; but maybe you shouldn't try it when you are behind the wheel or you could find yourself in something of a pickle, a bit like in the fable about the millipede that got his legs all tangled when he tried to understand how they worked when he walked.

Just as we can see the advantages of doing things on automatic, when we look back we can also see more clearly what the disadvantages are. We are only rarely aware of our automatic behaviors. As we get older, automatic routines and programs pile up in the brain. Many such programs are still there, stored up in memory and ready to spring into action, even if they have no role to play in our life anymore.

But automatic behavior mechanisms are not just passively waiting to be activated. Our brains are enormous storehouses of associations; and when a stored association fits a situation we find ourselves in, it kicks in – even if it is not at all a good fit and has long since lost its usefulness. And most of these mechanisms are not free of all feelings and emotions, like when you drive a car. Many of these automatic programs are emotionally charged. The feelings come with the reflexes, and from one moment to the next we become overwhelmed by our feelings and emotions.

Memories from childhood, for example, don't just stay with us for a long time – they also give rise to strong feelings. Maybe you remember an encounter that took place when you were little and you were frightened and felt powerless. You froze, nailed to the spot, but somehow you survived. And then what happens? Some association triggers the old program and we find ourselves right back there, frozen to the spot. This happens even though we are now grown up and the person in front of us is not a threat and we are certainly not helpless any more. But the program is running even though it doesn't at all apply to where we find ourselves now. Quite the contrary! And we find it irritating and confusing.

Can we free ourselves from our programming, in our everyday lives even? We can use the helpful programs; but how can we drop the ones that are triggered by an association and just run on automatically? For this you need awareness. Without awareness, we cannot even see that a program is running. This is astonishing! Give it a try. We manage to stay in the present and just observe the program that is running all on its own, and see that it has nothing to do with what is happening right now. When you do this, you throw a monkey wrench into the works. The automatic programs are on pause; but after a while, they get the upper hand and come back into play when the awareness is no longer present.

Let's look at an example: our memory summons up scenes of an annoying situation, perhaps even a conflict, that was never really resolved. We become aware of this and are astonished that this memory of anger long past makes itself felt in this body. It's perfectly clear that we can't do a thing about it and that our memories summon up pictures, a film of past events. The body quiets down. Now the old annoyances can come back as soon as our attention wanders. Suddenly we see what's happening: the old memories surge up with all the disruption they bring about in the body, and only a return to awareness will put a stop to the old program. So please: be patient! It can take a long time for these old habits to go and for programs that have been coming back for years maybe to finally quiet down.

In our everyday lives, when thoughts and feeling fill us up to the brim, there isn't much room left over for this kind of awareness. And our work-life is just one more complication in all this: our daily duties at work require us to be rational and function-oriented; and working with computers means that we can, and indeed we must, accomplish a great deal in a short period of time. Working like this means that we have to take care of many details and must think things through in order to not make any mistakes. It's like floodwater rising within, and we often find ourselves in the process of becoming completely overwhelmed.

Very few of us work with our hands or do work that gets done all on its own, like when we drive a car. We learn how something is done, muscle memory takes over and the mind is open and free to move about. Nowadays, simpler trades and handicrafts are done mostly by machines. The modern workplace means that we have to carry out very concentrated intellectual tasks. When our attention and intellectual faculties are focused and fully active, only then can we operate modern machinery or do computer work. Little wonder that there are more and more cases of people who feel overwhelmed by their jobs, and why there are so many cases of burnout and of people suffering from depression.

This is something we really have to understand: our daily lives are so thoroughly organized that there is hardly any free time left over to pause and look, and become aware of what is happening within us and around us. We run on automatic pilot so that we can somehow stay on top of everything: we are controlled by the program running within. We're often stressed out, but we're so completely taken up with things that have to be done that we can't see the programs and structures that give rise to this feeling of unease.

Is it possible to carefully observe our own stress when it comes up in the moment? Mind you, it's hard to slow down and pause like this in the middle of a busy, stressful day. Looking back in a quiet moment, when time permits, is much easier. When we are stressed out, our body is excited out of all proportion by programming that is getting us ready for "flight or fight".

Our body is getting ready to exert itself to the max, but almost no movement is required. Computer work is the task or sitting and talking. When our bodies are always in a state of high alert and stays that way hour after hour, the stress can end up making us sick.

Our body is used to being activated and then calming down once things have quieted down again. Actually, alternating between periods of activity and respite is healthy and even conducive to our well-being. We wouldn't be happy if our lives were always flat with no ups or downs. We're happiest when we have our ups and downs, and tense moments of stress are followed by the release of tension. But when we have days when there is no let up from the stress, we never get a moment's respite, and cannot even sleep at night – this has consequences. In the truest sense of the word, we have a burn-out: we get depressed and the body shuts down.

At the firm where I work, the team leader of one of the groups gave everything up overnight and took a year's sick leave. In the course of his year off, he underwent therapy. It seemed to do him a world of good. He came back to work, to his old job. But after a short while he told us that he found himself back in the old rut he thought he had finally left. He handed in his notice and left the company.

I don't know if it's possible to dismantle structures that give rise to stress, and reduce the burdensome work load of those we work with. Not to say that it can't be done, but many of those involved – our fellow workers, the administration and those in charge – must recognize that there is a problem and that the people working there feel pressured.

Not everyone is necessarily stressed out: some people are almost always happy where they work, and others just can't stand it, and they're doing the same job. Maybe my colleague at work was having family troubles as well; maybe he had a long commute into work in the morning. Maybe he just didn't have what it took. Then we say that he doesn't know how to go with the flow!

How can we become resilient and learn how to fight back against stress? What is it that makes it possible for us to avoid stress and not make ourselves sick with worry about what has to be done? We've already said that stress is the inner state of an over-active body and that it doesn't come from our surroundings or where we find ourselves, like at work. Can we somehow avoid getting stressed out when we find ourselves in a stressful situation?

And here we come back to awareness. When we see in the moment that we are becoming physically stressed, that our thinking is all over the place and that we're mentally stressed out – is it possible to just drop everything, just for a moment? Why do we act so blindly in stressful situations? It is so because we blindly go along with the inner movements of the mind. When we are able to perceive in the moment, as it is happening, that the stress is arising within, then we have already made progress. If it can happen in retreat, then maybe it can happen when you find yourself at work.

It is possible for us to see how many programs are automatically running within, is it not? When we're sitting in front of the computer at work and have to carry out some complicated task, thoughts are running through the mind already. Are we trying to solve several problems at once? Parallel streams of thoughts and feelings flow through us; they drain us of the very energy we need for our job. We often feel that our job is exhausting and hard to do; but in reality, we are not just working at our job: we are also taken up with these parallel processes. Is it possible for us to pause in the midst of what we are doing at work, and to make this a habit? Is it possible to look, time and again, to see what is happening within? Astonishingly, moments of waking up come time and again, one after the other, even at work. Such moments are often fleeting, because we are already lost in the next program, the next stream of thought. But when we realize the importance of these moments of waking up, then other such moments of insight and stillness might occur.

That's what happens with me, even at work: there's a moment of waking up. Suddenly I'm face to face with everything that's going on within. Often as not, what I see is not always constructive or joyful; "My back hurts, I feel so very tired; I'm bogged down at work" – but there is a moment of insight. Even though I don't always want to see what's there, I don't just pass over the moment. Instead, I pause for a short while; maybe just look out the window. It might not be very nice out. Maybe it's one of those grey, drizzly days that makes you feel down. Maybe disturbing thoughts come up one after another: "I can't finish this project today. How am I going to meet the deadline?" Pleasant or unpleasant: can we see all of this happening in our everyday lives and wake up to what is happening?

The body needs some time to quiet down, more than just a few seconds. It takes a couple of minutes for our stress level to go down. Is it possible to just be aware and stay in the here and now, in this little space of time; and realize that there are just too many things happening all at once? Often, our awareness is full to overflowing with every-thing that's going on around us, and with programs and processes going on inside. At such times it is very difficult indeed, and a great challenge to become aware and to re-main so for even a little space of time. This doesn't always work; but there are still those brief moments of awareness that come up again and again, and there is a chance that such moment will last long enough for the body to calm down.

When we have had this experience more than once, and see that waking up in awareness bring with it release of stress and tension, then we learn to treasure those mo-ments and we no longer fear what is seen so clearly. It is easier to become aware now, at the end of a retreat. Maybe you have already experienced this release of tension in mind and body, when for a short while there is awareness; maybe you have already learned to treasure such mo-ments. . . The body can learn. Then, in our everyday lives, there exists the possibility that there will be a moment of awareness that will linger; and when we are awake to what is happening, we have the freedom to focus on just what is before us. We clearly see that too much is just too much and say, "Enough is enough!" How much easier our job becomes when the mind is clear and we can concentrate on one task at a time!

We are often unaware of what we are saying to others; our meaning is not always clear, and this in itself gives rise to a great deal of stress. We communicate with others in an automatic fashion because the mind is overwhelmed. Is it possible to really listen to the person you're talking to? This is what makes for good communication, a satisfying exchange between two people. Listening in this manner means really hearing what the other person is saying, but also paying attention to what we are saying ourselves. Is it possible to listen to our own words, and to be attentive to the feelings and thoughts that arise as we speak?

And hearing what those who are closest to us are saying is perhaps the most difficult of all. Over the long years of living with someone in a relationship, we become programmed and develop so many habits and repetitive ways of relating to each other that open listening becomes nearly impossible.

Which reminds me of what sometimes happens at home. I often speak to my wife about things we have to do at home, like "You can make the salad" or "You could at least read that letter!" And she answers right back: "You don't always have to tell me what to do!" Often as not, a simple glance tells me that she already wants to do what I'm asking her to do, or has even already started to do it. My wife gets worked up because I behave as though it went without saying that she needs extra instructions. In the moment – at that moment – we are acting out of habit. For my part, I speak from the desire to get something organized, when I can see at a glance that this is already being done;

and on my wife's side, anger because I give her instructions that are neither necessary nor appropriate. But what is really nice is when neither of us take this scripted program seriously when it starts again.

When we both become aware of what is happening and we've talked it through, there's a change – what is meant and heard and what gives rise to anger: this is all clearly seen, and when it happens again we can't help but to laugh at it all. We both know that this is old stuff, a program running all on its own, and we don't have to take it seriously any more. And it seems to me that it doesn't happen as often as it used to . . .

How do we communicate with people at work? What strikes me most about so-called professional communication is this: it is formal and functional. We like to say we're talking facts and figures, but what does this really mean? Talking facts means we have forgotten the human side of communication. Talking facts and figures often means that we see the people at work like part of a computer program: data in, data out. It's all about function.

In the midst of all our busy-ness, is it possible to observe what goes on in us and realize how we communicate, also at the working place? How does the person in front of us feel? Do we have the sensitivity to sense how someone else is feeling? Is our inborn empathy and ability to read the emotions of others alive and active? Or is it just shut down because we are stressed out and overwhelmed by all the work we have to get done, so there is no room left for us to be aware of people's feelings? It doesn't make much of a difference whether you're in administration or just a regular employee; in either case, purely functional communication excludes the human element. The person in front of us is suddenly no longer a human being with feelings and emotions, but just a cog in the machine. People treated like this feel they're being used; but when we're not on the receiving end ourselves, we rationalize our behavior. We like to say, "We're professionals and we have to be able to take the heat." But no one wants to work for a company where they will be treated just like another cog in the machine.

How do you communicate with people at work? In my case it isn't always that easy. There are often moments when things get tense. Sometimes I'm just wiped out and don't have any energy left after dealing with the many matters that come up in the course of a busy workday. And then someone shows up with a complaint; and suddenly the energy is there, like when an alarm goes off. Can we direct this burst of energy into seeing rather than becoming angry? Is it possible to disrupt our usual way of reacting to a complaint and just ask ourselves what is actually happening at that moment?

I've made it a habit at work to start out by inviting the person in front of me to sit down at my round worktable. I look at them without saying anything and I take a moment to reflect, to look at what is happening within, and already there is a lot taking place. In that brief moment an emotional link is created between me and the person seated across from me, who can also be still and quiet for a moment.

When we're excited and all worked up, we just barge ahead; but when we just sit back and take a moment to be quiet and still, there is a real chance to tackle the problem that has arisen – but in a factual manner so that no one is just a cog in the machine. Is it possible to look at a problem together with someone when you're at the office and quietly discuss what can be done, or see if a solution is even possible? The answer is yes, you can.

Granted, I have my own office and a round table for meeting with people in addition to my desk; so maybe that's why I get along so well with my colleagues. But perhaps you too can find a way to have these exchanges with people at work.

It's possible, even at work, to take a moment to be quiet and look inward before words rise to the lips. When there is awareness, which we cultivate when we are in retreat, that is in itself useful; but when we don't make use of it in our everyday lives, then we are not making use of the full potential of awareness. I encourage you to bring awareness into your everyday life. Make it part and parcel of your everyday encounters. Without it, we enter into conflict with others because we act blindly and thoughtlessly.

I have one other aspect of our work life to discuss, namely how we identify with roles. This is also something that always results in unnecessary stress. In many businesses there's what we call a soft hierarchy, where from the outside it looks like everyone is the same; but on the inside people are fighting to get ahead, to get to see who will be boss. These are structures that cause stress and uncertainty and give rise to power struggles.

Not everyone has a say in how things are done at this place of work; but when decisions have to be made, it helps when roles and responsibilities are clearly defined. How things are done at work should not be a question of who has authority: the various jobs and tasks that have to be carried out must be given to those who are best qualified to do the work. A clear administrative structure and hierarchy, and divvying up the workload based on the abilities of each and every employee, makes things easier for everyone.

When everyone knows what they have to do and knows what everyone else's job is too, then communication becomes a lot easier. Constant controls and checks are no longer necessary. Take a look at where you work. Are things done in an orderly manner? Is it a place where you want to spend most of your waking hours?

Sometimes you have to leave your place of work and find a job elsewhere; when, for example, you see that things are chaotic and disorganized and that this puts even more of a burden on the people working there. And when I see that I am just a cog in the machine and that there is no room to be creative, maybe it's time to realize that a change is needed, whatever problems and uncertainties that may bring.

I find it helpful when I'm on my way to work in the morning to look and see how I feel. When I see that I'm looking forward to going into work, even though it can sometimes be stressful and brings with it problems and disappointment – but still, I look forward to going in – I take this as a sign to stay where I am. There was a time when I had to force myself to go into work, but that didn't last very long. I went to work elsewhere, and I was amazed how everything just fell into place once I realized that I couldn't stay on with the other company.

But enough talk about work! Most of us just go back home after a day's work. Maybe we're just wiped and de-stress in front of the TV or get lost on the internet.

I've reached the point where I hardly ever watch TV any more, apart from the news every now and then. My evenings are given over to meditation or exercise. Sports I find very important. When I spend the whole livelong day doing intellectual work, I feel the need to move and use my body, to do something physical.

I don't meditate at home very often. I find it very helpful to belong to a local meditation group. We meet once a week, on Tuesday evenings, and sit for three twenty-five-minute rounds with five-minute breaks between rounds, just like in retreat. At the end we have group dialogue, and anyone can bring up any subject they wish.

In my experience, the stillness and the silence of a sitting that takes place at the end of a workday is only rarely like the quiet and stillness in retreat. Thoughts about work often intrude, since feelings arise from work and the events of the day are still fresh in the mind. Sometimes these streams of thought run the full course and there is a lot of inner noise. We are harboring false expectations when we say to ourselves that we're going to sit down and enter into deep stillness. This hardly ever happens to me on Tuesday evenings. But when I have no expectations and just quietly look within, then I can see what is going on. It's the same as being in retreat; the content of the mind is different.

This is why the group is so valuable: I can get together and meditate with others and I have the space and the time to quietly look at what happens in the course of my workday or at whatever may come up. After the sitting we have our little group dialogue and we always have an intense and wide-ranging discussion. People speak of what they have seen and they have come to understand. Sometimes they share very personal information with the group. We've become a warm and welcoming little community where I feel very much at home.

The second group I belong to meets once a month on a Sunday afternoon. We sit for five rounds with a tea-break in the middle. My job no longer intrudes that much on my weekends; and during our sittings, I experience moments of deep silence more often. Most of the time I come home from our Sunday sittings calm and refreshed, and other members of the group say the same thing: they feel refreshed and rested after our afternoon together.

If you can be part of a meditation group that has regular sittings, I highly recommend that you do so. It's easier to sit quietly for a longer period when you're with a group.

Some people have told me that sitting at home twice a day, in the morning and evening, has become part of their regular routine; but this is not easy to do. I tried doing this some years ago. I thought: easy. I just get up an hour earlier so I can sit for an hour. But I ended up nodding off for an hour because I was too tired, and there was no awareness possible. It just didn't work. My wife and I have worked out a different routine, and we've been doing this for a while now: we have breakfast and then a good cup of strong coffee and we sit for ten or twenty minutes before going to work. This works much better for us.

We, each of us, have to see what works best; and we all have different daily routines and times during the day when we are most awake and alert. Everyone has a time during the day that is best for meditation. Meditating on your own is often hard to do, even if you have a set daily routine with time set aside to meditate. It's much easier to meditate with other like-minded people, together. They're meditators too, and this alone is encouraging and supportive. We're social creatures. When we sit together in stillness and silence, a shared energy makes itself felt: this is the energy of seeing, of looking inward, and it is not always there when you sit alone.

Does sitting regularly make it easier for us to be aware? See for yourself! Is there something happening? Does it become easier to pause during the day and just be still and look inward? You shouldn't have high hopes, but when you look back after a few years, you will see, something has changed in your life.

I noticed an unexpected change many years ago in the way I talked with people: I found that there was a new kind of attentiveness present when meeting people face to face. There were more often moments when there was room, not only to truly listen to the person speaking, but also space to see my own thoughts and feelings.

Indeed, our everyday life is hardly a day of retreat, and our heads are full of a thousand and one thoughts; but even in our everyday life, there are moments when we can be still and quiet and look inwards. Then we have the space to see and do not always have to act blindly. The longer we meditate, the more likely and the easier it becomes for us to make use of these moments of awakening. Our body learns; and being still and quiet and looking inwards, aware of what is taking place within – this becomes part of our daily life and experience. Little by little, meditation becomes more than formal rounds of sitting; and then one day, we realize that our life has been transformed.

Postscript

In the last forty years of meditation work – forty years already! – the practice of awareness has greatly evolved. In this postscript, I would like to describe my own experiences and recognize the role played by Toni Packer in all of this. She is the founder of this way of meditation, and it is to her that I owe much of my own development.

In the 1980's, with Sabine who was later to become my wife, I met Toni Packer in Hamburg in the course of a seven-day retreat in Roseburg. I still thought that I was getting involved with authentic Rinzai Zen. I later learned that Toni had left the Rochester Zen Center in 1981 and, free of the strictures of Zen Buddhism, had developed her own way of meditating.

By 1983 she had already dropped the endless bowing and the chanting of sacred Buddhist texts, but some people still wanted to work with koans. These are short, often paradoxical stories that are part of the Zen tradition. There was still the kyosaku (a flat stick), and people sitting in meditation could ask to be struck on the shoulders; this was supposed to help release tension and focus the attention.

Very carefully, gingerly, after twenty years had gone by (ten years of which were given over to her Zen practice), she developed a new way of meditating. Many people came with her and took part in this long and slow process: they all played a role. Truth be told, everyone in the group helped bring this about. The kyosaku was dropped in the 80's already. I don't remember anyone kicking up a fuss or saying that they missed the stick.

It was a joy to be part of this whole process. Once I began working with Toni, real Zen didn't arouse much interest anymore. I never had a Zen practice, so I am in no position to make any value judgements.

As I began to regularly help out as retreat coordinator in her German retreats, I clearly remember Toni saying towards the end of the 90's: "This way of doing things works very well. I don't want to make any other changes." I was of the same opinion. Form and content were one; they worked perfectly for our mediation work, for all of us as a group, in Germany and in beautiful Springwater.

Over the years, it has become easier and easier for coordinators to organize retreats. Many details seem to fall into place on their own. In the early years, for example, we had to work it out so that the line of people waiting to go in and speak with Toni didn't have to sit for too long. We hit upon just making a list. People who wanted to speak with her privately signed up on a list with set times. There was a schedule. The days of retreat go by in silence and simplicity. Everyone contributes to the stillness and the silence. We ended up creating space where people could meditate in silence, alone or with others; no pressure.

Toni didn't require people to come to her talks or to speak with her privately. It was a matter of choice, and she made this very clear. She was very much aware that as the head of a meditation center, she would at once be held up as an authority figure, as someone who wanted to be believed and understood, no questions asked. I can't remember taking part in a single seven-day retreat in which she did not bring up the question of authority on opening evening, stressing that she was not a teacher with students. She was not at all a teacher in the traditional sense of the word: the work of meditation can only flourish and bloom when people work together in a balanced and attentive manner, when nothing is taken at face value as being right and true.

In speaking with people privately and also in the group dialogues that came into being later on, she would often say: "Let us look at this with fresh eyes!" In these two ways of speaking with one another, that go hand in hand, it became possible for us to carefully look into the meaning of words and concepts, and together come to an intellectual and emotional understanding of what was being said.

I still remember how, in my early seven-day retreats, I would sit waiting in line to go in to speak with Toni; and, with thumping heart, wonder what I would say to her. Later, I would go in calm of mind and without any expectations. There was a lovely feeling of freedom in these retreats. Whatever subject I brought up in private meetings, could unfold effortlessly.

The slow and thoughtful evolution of the seven-day retreats that I went through in Germany at the same time, took place with a special intensity at Springwater Center in New York State, that Toni founded with a group of like-minded people after she left the Rochester Zen Center. With great enthusiasm, a lot of know-how, hard work and personal commitment, a meditation center was built out in the countryside about fifty miles from Rochester.

The floor had not yet been laid in the dining room when I first went to Springwater, but the work of meditation had already begun. My first seven-day silent retreat there was a revelation to me. I was welcomed with open arms, and even though my English was not up to scratch, I felt very much at home.

This was the first of my yearly trips to Springwater. I love going there, and especially enjoy my quiet walks in the woods and through the fields. The Center consists of a big new building on a piece of land that was once a farm. All the land is Center property. Nature has taken over the farmland and you can walk for miles through the fields and along the trails through the woods. You get see white-tailed deer! They love grazing in the big meadows there, where hunting is forbidden.

When I am at Springwater, I like to sit up by the pond on a solid little bench. Toni liked things to be solid. I sit there and meditate with the croaking frogs and the screeching red-winged blackbirds. When they take flight, you can see the flash of red on the underside of their wings.

After Toni's death, the question came up of how the Center would carry on without her. She had always rejected the notion of Dharma-heirs, where "senior people"/students who were given permission to teach by the teacher would carry on the work. But she did name people. These were people who had decades of meditation work behind them. They were encouraged to become active because she felt they would be able to carry on the work of the Center.

These people [5] took on responsibility. Together with the Springwater staff and the many who regularly came and continued to come to retreats and events, they preserved the center and are continuously developing it.

---

[5] I am the only one carrying on Toni's work in Europe; all the others live in the U.S.

Several retreat leaders have developed their own style of retreat. For example, Quiet Weeks [6] are held at Springwater: a relatively small number of people come together for two weeks or more to meditate and take part in daily group meetings. These regular group meetings, over a period of time, make possible a deeper and more intense exchange among participants, as people learn to trust one another.

Unfortunately, I have not had the chance to take part in these new ways of meditation, since I can only be there once a year to lead my own retreat.

I am most thankful to everyone in Springwater for their support for the work I do here in Europe, but I am even more pleased that I am invited back to Springwater to lead seven-day retreats. For me, Springwater is the ideal setting for my meditation work to flourish; a place where all the heavy lifting, from preparing for the retreat right down to the mealtimes, is done by the Springwater staff.

I lead seven-day retreats in two European countries, following the week-long format Toni developed. These retreats are very much like the ones held at Springwater.

For many years now, I have been holding retreats in Poland also. Jacek Dobrowolski was a student of Toni's at the Rochester Center. He is an outstanding interpreter and translator of all my talks into Polish [7]. My first seven-day

---

[6] Sandra Gonzalez began the Quiet Weeks form of meditation. She also leads retreats at her center in Nicaragua. You can find more information about her retreats on the Springwater website. The contact addresses are at the end of the book.

[7] German retreatants who know English are most welcome to come to the Polish retreats!

retreat with Jacek took place in Warsaw in 2004. Toni had recommended that I take over from Dagmar Apel, who had been leading retreats in Poland for many years but was no longer doing this [8]. It was quite the adventure for me not to be working in my mother tongue! But as I was meditating on the flight to Warsaw, a sense of certainty settled over me, and the retreat went very smoothly. I was invited back the next year, and I have been back almost every year since then.

For more than ten years now I have been leading retreats in Germany, in German. Even under the Corona restrictions, we held a live retreat in 2020 (although there were fewer participants); but the Springwater and Poland retreats were held online.

As I am writing the last few sentences of this book, spring is here and the pandemic is on the way out. I just learned that Springwater is welcoming back a small number of vaccinated visitors. That gives one hope, does it not? I look forward to spending the next seven days in silence with you all, alone and also in community with you. This is indeed wonderful!

---

[8] Please see the reference to Dagmar Apel's book in the bibliography at the end of the book.

Recommended Books and Contacts

A book can sometimes inspire us to do something, or to want to do something; but we lose track of title and author and after a while our enthusiasm just peters out.

To remedy this, I've made a list of book titles and authors and contact information you may turn to, to further explore the practice of meditation rooted in silence, stillness and simple awareness.

I lead two meditation groups in Northern Germany. We meet regularly, once a month in Hamburg on a Sunday afternoon, and once a week in Elmshorn. If you speak some German, you can find more information at my website www.springwater-meditation.de. Also on the website, you can find information about the week-long retreats I lead in German and in English that take place in Germany, Poland and at the Springwater Center in the United States. More information about my retreat in Springwater and retreats offered there by other teachers can be found on the Springwater website, www.springwatercenter.org.

The books listed here in the bibliography are all original in English language. Also German versions of Toni Packers books exist but are translations. If you want to meditate as you read, then I recommend these books to you with all my heart.

Toni's books, up to The Silent Question, can be found on the internet and at book stores. They all can be ordered directly from the Springwater Center www.springwater-center.org.

The titles of the original English editions of Toni's books are listed below:

The Work of this Moment

The Light of Discovery

The Wonder of Presence

The Silent Question

Seeing without knowing and A retreat Dialogue cannot be found on the internet or at book stores. It can be ordered directly from www.springwatercenter.org.

You can find a series of talks given by Toni Packer in German, and many more in English, on YouTube. I also have videos of talks on YouTube, some in English and some in German; and there are talks available by other Springwater teachers in English. You can find all of these videos using 'Springwater Center" as a key word or in a name search.

I would like to recommend two books in English by authors who are well acquainted with meditating in this open manner, with a focus on awareness:

Buddha's Flower, Newton's Apple - Dagmar Apel's book describes her experience meditating in the Zen tradition and also in the open way of meditating taught by Toni Packer. She now focusses on non-duality in her meditation work and observes non-duality from the point of view of the natural sciences.

Once is so Many - Robert Watson's book is a volume of poetry. Many of the texts in this book he wrote in Springwater, being in retreat or during stays at the Center.

Bibliography

Apel, Dagmar: Buddha's Flower – Newton's Apple. One Person's Enlightenment in a Material World. Bronxville, NY, 2016

Packer, Toni: Fragen in der Stille. Meditieren jenseits des Wissens. Einführung von Stephan Bielfeldt. Bielefeld 2007

Packer, Toni: Mit ganz neuen Augen sehen. Braunschweig 1991

Packer, Toni: The Light of Discovery. Boston, London 2007

Packer, Toni: Der Moment der Erfahrung ist unendlich. Meditation jenseits von Tradition und Methode. Berlin 1996

Packer, Toni: A Retreat Dialog with Toni Packer. A Group Dialog which Took Place on Day Three of the September 2004 Retreat at Springwater Center. Springwater 2005

Packer, Toni: Seeing without Knowing. What is Meditative Inquiry? Springwater 1995

Packer, Toni: The Silent Question. Meditating in the Stillness of Not-Knowing. Boston, London 2007

Packer, Toni: The Wonder of Presence and the Way of Meditative Inquiry. Boston, London 2002

Packer, Toni: The Work of this Moment. Vermont, Tokyo 1990

Packer, Toni: The Work of this Moment. Boston 2007

Watson, Robert G.: Once is so Many. Victoria BC 2019

About the Author

Stephan has been doing meditation work and holding retreats in both German and English since 2003.

He started working with Toni Packer in 1983, regularly taking part in her retreats in Germany and in the United States. Towards the end of 1990, Toni asked him to offer private meetings with participants during her retreats in Germany.

In 2003, she asked that he lead retreats in Poland and in Germany; and since that time, he has been holding retreats regularly in German and in English. He has helped to found two meditation groups. Interested people may join the regular meetings of these groups live or online, which bring together people in Germany and abroad.

Beginning in 1986, when Stephan first visited Springwater Center in the USA, he has come almost every year to participate in a retreat. In 2010, he began holding retreats at Springwater and comes back whenever his time allows it. "I was most fortunate to have been able to work closely with Toni Packer for so many years. I seek to share with others the experience and insights of those years of meditation work, in retreat and in the meditation groups."

Stephan lives in northern Germany, near the city of Hamburg. In his daily life, he is an engineer. For him, it is of utter importance that professional life and meditative life can unfold together in harmony.